A Notch Above Novice

by Robin Olivero

Edited by Judy King

2014

Preface

When I began the "Life Lessons" adventure four years ago, I never imagined my life would be as it is now. Though these books have been fun and were intended to be a gift of personal insight for family and friends, it fulfilled a lifelong goal—to be an author. Writers, though many well-spoken, tend to express themselves best in the written word. I find clarity when I write and peace when I complete a thought, be it long or short.

The last few months of 2013 presented many challenges; while I've gained a lot, it proved to be the year of loss for me. Three of the four most important males in my life have been removed and left me with holes where I once felt complete.

My father's passing, though the best thing for him under the circumstances in which he lived, has removed the protective "daddy look" I could see in his eyes. There were five of us girls growing up, and we were each daddy's little girl in our own unique way. I will always be his little tomboy girl, but how I miss those eyes watching over me from a comforting view. I know he sees me, but I miss seeing him. The life I now live and love was greatly influenced by the time I spent with my dad growing up; from bucking bronco rides on his knee, my first Marvel the Mustang, and the numerous hours we spent watching John Wayne movies. I'm still amazed when I find myself loving every minute spent in the middle of 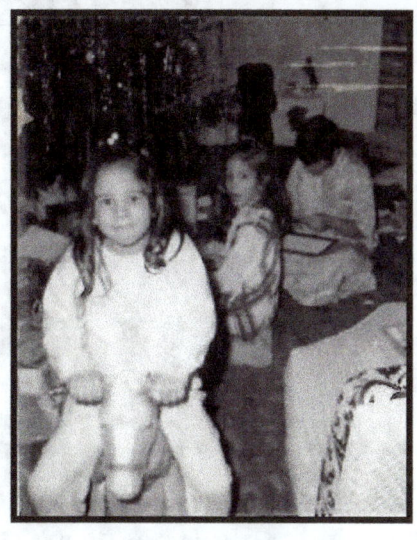 the desert on a horse. I am very thankful for those formative years spent with Dad. When my older sisters were out and about and I was "stuck" at home, little did I know then it was preparing me for a life I live now.

After moving to the "Wild West" I finally let someone in, someone I believed understood me, loved me beyond outside appearances, and filled me with a future hope I had never known. After almost four year, that ceased to be and I felt hopeless. As to what happened and why, I am not certain, and I am learning I may never know. These "Life Lessons" contain a lot of content that I learned during this relationship. There are things I learned personally and through observing his life, despite his attempts to keep me from feeling the effects of his issues. One of the hardest lessons of all was learning that no matter how well you think you know someone, you never really do. In the mere seconds it takes for the truth to be revealed (and it will always come out), your life can change forever.

The final loss of 2013 can be found in this book. As timing would have it, I couldn't move forward with editing and publishing for the strangest reasons until now. It all became clear and you will see why in my final entry of Life Lessons (but try not to peek ahead). Though there is still so much to learn, life has a funny way of continuing with its twists and turns, and I am continuing to ride on and embrace new life lessons.

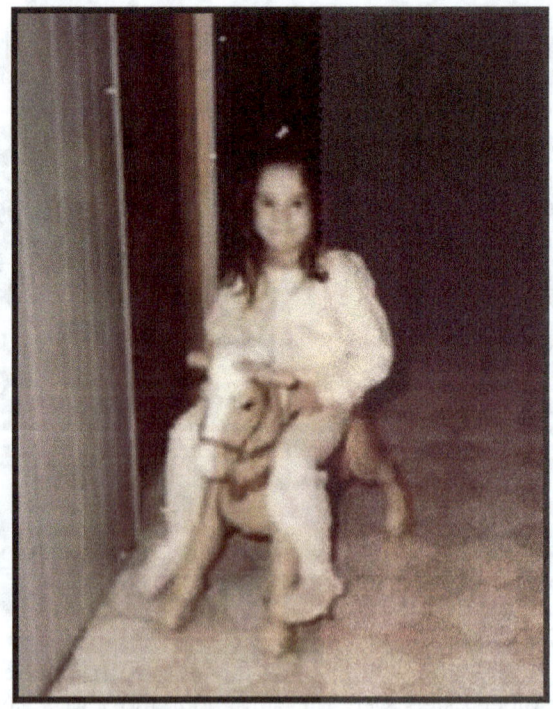

"Life is like an endless trail that leads to the unknown. You can embrace the adventure believing something better is ahead or settle for less than what awaits you."

❧ Robin Olivero

Home

I must clear something up....I admittedly utilize modern-day technology and enjoy some of life's conveniences and comforts but, yes, the rumors are true....I have gone "country." I wear cowboy boots and Levi's, and I like country music. I love that dressing up means gals in sundresses and guys in their best boots, clean Levi's, and a faint smell of Skoal and beer lingering from their day of working at the ranch. I love the mid-paced, drama-free world of rock- and cactus-ridden mountains, and the peace of desert sunrises and sunsets. I love the stillness and quiet of the desert, where phones and computers are replaced with quiet company and where there are no cars, buses, or loud radios, just the sounds of animals running free and the breaths you breathe. I love the smell of my horse and the hard work it takes to care for him. I love the way people get up early and do their daily chores before heading to work and then come home to do them again after work. I find solace in the simplicity of the most beautiful scenery nature provides. I enjoy having a small wardrobe with only a few shoes to choose from and the way people are more concerned about their loved ones and animals than the way they look or who likes them. I enjoy the sound of an acoustic guitar with a country-twanged singer in the background of everything I do, and the way people can dance with each other just for fun.

Yes, I've gone country and found values I've seen only in John Wayne movies growing up. I appreciate men who genuinely respect and treat women with the basic consideration every human being deserves...opening doors for you as you walk in before them, saying "thank you" and "have a good day" as they tip their hat when you walk past them. I appreciate women out here who smell like their horse's fly spray and not $100 perfume, whose hair is a mess, yet they are at peace with who they are and what they have. I love these women who befriend you simply because you're human; they are not jealous of what you have because they are content with what they have. Yes, we have dance clubs, shopping malls, and fine dining, but not often will you find these people there. You will see them at rodeos, ranches, or in the open desert landscape. It isn't perfect where I am because people are not perfect, but it's the perfect home for me.

Although I still suit up for the corporate world Monday through Friday, I can't wait each week to escape those four walls. I love the sights, sounds, smells, and, most of all, the simplicity of country. I am still me, but I am happiest at home, and my definition of "home" has radically changed since moving away from the suburbs of Chicago. I may not have much of what others view as valuable, but I've chosen this life and feel richly blessed.....I have more than I need, and there is no other place on earth I'd rather be.

Catch and Release

There was a pivotal point between Jr and me when we "captured the moment" and cleared a barrier. Before this moment, we'd had many great rides, but now I can see that he had been merely compliant up to that point. It was like he had been testing my commitment to him. There are many ways a horse can give you attitude to test you. Jr's favorite has always been the "I'll just stop and stand here and see how much you push me to move" method. That stopped after I got spurs, but then he started the head-throwing, bucking, and rearing method. There were also many moments of "let's ride sideways on the trail just so I'm not going forward like you want me to." Finally, there was the "I'm going to make you think I'm about to go crazy and run at top speed so you'll turn around and take me home" method. That one was especially interesting.

On that pivotal day, Jr and I set out on a trail ride alone, and he pretty much tried every single method, but none of them worked. I finally got to a point where I was so angry that he just wouldn't freakin' chill out and enjoy the ride! I stuck to my guns, got pissed, and simply told him, "We ARE going to do this thing!" I just wanted to spend some time alone with him without all the horse games. Geesh . . . (deep sigh). Then without anticipating it, I could feel his body just release. He "broke," he just gently released whatever it was that prevented him from fully connecting and flowing with me. Every ride since then has been a dance, with a synergy that we didn't have before. Don't get me wrong, the affection between us had always been there and it was obvious to everyone. But this new connection goes far beyond what you can see. One lifelong horsewoman told me, "What happened is Jr now trusts you. Whatever happened to him before you began riding him could have prevented him from fully trusting you, but now he gets it."

Let's face it, we all have trust issues at some level. We've all been hurt and we create that internal barrier as a means of self-preservation. We all test each other's commitment level when we enter a relationship, and I believe that's healthy. However, in order for the relationship to fully develop, there has to come a point when we release whatever past baggage causes us to test that person and just enjoy the ride. I do believe that trust on any level should be earned, but I also believe we should recognize where the line is when the other person has proven worthy of our trust. You know, that line when you stop second-guessing every good deed and kind word to see if there's a selfish, underlying motive. If you realize your toes never come to that line, you have two choices: either release those people from your testing method and your life, or buck up and realize that with trust there is always a risk of being let down. We're human, we fail each other. Just be wise with what is simple, realistic with what is expected, and remember that trust works both ways.

The Dance

With riding, it's interesting how there comes a moment where it all clicks and feels right. In that moment, the control of your horse and the flow of the moment perfectly collide and you feel like you and your horse are dancing as opposed to riding. That moment is unexplainable; you cannot create it, anticipate it, or even prepare for it; it just happens. All the hours of shoveling poop, grooming, and taking rides when you're scared out of your mind overcoming your fear are all a part of the investment needed to find yourself in that moment. It's as if time stands still and you connect with your four-legged companion on a level beyond earthly understanding. What is amazing about this experience is the feeling that the ones before it all seemed like the best it would ever be. And, then, you have one even better. Amazing. You cherish all of those moments and savor the incomprehensible feeling you have, which is certainly part of the reason we horse lovers continue to take the bumps and lumps we face in the battle of the wills between ourselves and our horse.

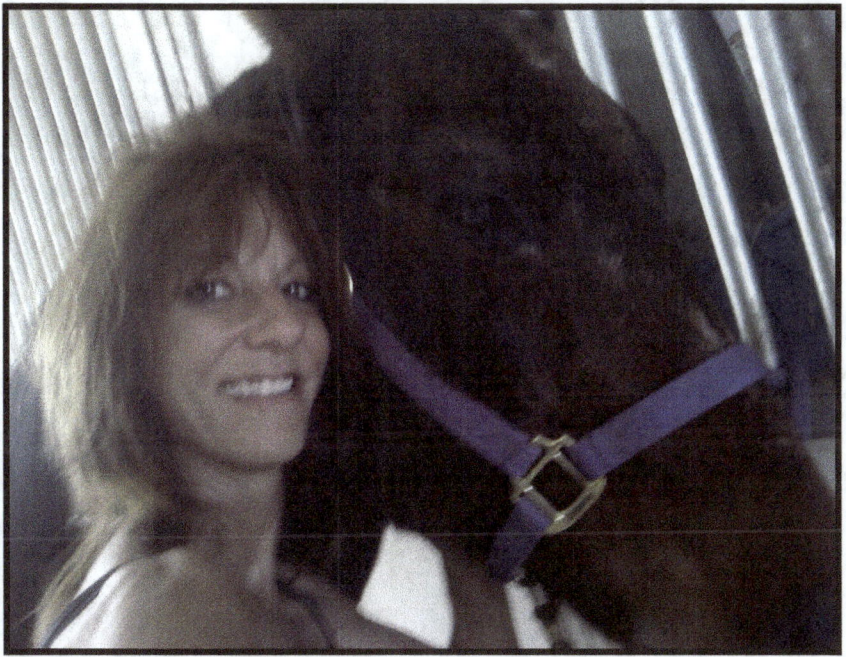

When life suddenly changes the beat and you miss a step, it's certainly easier to stop dancing through the moment and find yourself stuck in the chorus, repeating the same stanza over and over again. It's interesting how those growth-inducing moments can challenge the comfort of our stagnation. There is a certain comfort we humans find in immobility and unproductivity, even when things are at their worst. Change is difficult because it means we have to adjust internally to flow with our outward circumstances. Human nature resists the unfamiliar, and even unpleasant familiar, feelings when change disrupts the moment of here and now. It means we have to make a decision to ride out that change until things settle into normality (whatever that is), or buck against it until we reach the point of exhaustion and just accept what is.

Just as I can no longer call myself a novice rider, neither can I consider myself completely unknowing about life. Though I am youthful in my approach to life and live it to the fullest, I've been through enough to know that every change I must face presents an opportunity for growth. Growing pains are a part of life. Though I am still just half a notch above novice, I am growing, and the investment I make will produce yet more moments to cherish and savor in this thing we call life. Sometimes we have to just go through the motions and do what we must do. But if we capture what is just for us in that moment, we find that this life has so much more to offer than we often give it credit for. Yes, there is pain, a lot of it, but in the midst of what seems like misery and emotional chaos, there is a peace no outside influence can disrupt. I have found this place many times by stilling myself, looking inward, and remembering that my life is not what happens to me, but rather *how I chose to live it*. I can either remain at a standstill as the beat picks up, or pick myself up and dance to the new rhythm.

"A dog looks up to a man,
A cat looks down on a man,
But a patient horse looks a man in the
eye and sees him as an equal."

Unknown

Social Graces

On one of our long horseback journeys, two other companions and I set out with a destination in mind, but had never actually traveled by horse to get there. We had no real idea about what we would encounter; we simply set out knowing only that we'd go through some desert parks, hills, valleys, and a few streets. After several hours of exploring some rigorous trails, we arrived near some houses. Well, actually we were in someone's backyard. In fact, once we hit pavement, we came to realize this wasn't your average neighborhood; it was some high-society, country-club neighborhood next to a golf course! All I could do was laugh. The homeowner of the yard we came through did laugh at

our directionally challenged moment as our fearless leader approached him. Terri and I just hung back, giggling at how utterly silly we must have looked. We got our trotting orders to get to a street we recognized, and of course this pavement path took us right down the street a mile or two through this fancy neighborhood. The funny thing about horses is they have no idea what social class and proper etiquette are. Here we are, sweaty, sun-kissed crispy, and dusty from the ride, and as we go along our merry little way, our horses basically behaved like horses. As Mercedes and Beamers passed us, Jr and his buddies left their version of "Jr and company were here." All I could do was laugh; I certainly wasn't prepared to dismount and clean up after him. I actually don't think they make travel-size pooper scoopers for horses.

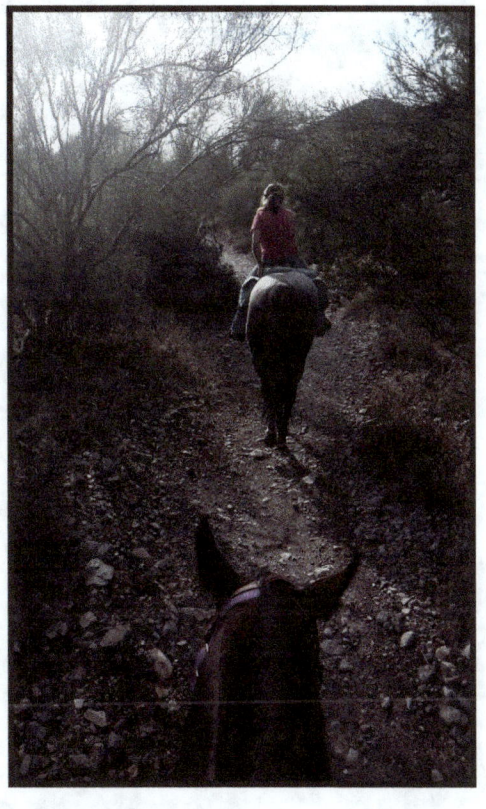

Isn't it funny how some people alter who they are and what they do to fit in? They change what they wear, say, drive, and even aspire to be, all to have some social status that somehow defines who they are. I find great humor in the whole experience because I am keenly aware of how some people look up or down their noses. The reality is, we are all just people. We all carry in our bodies a heart, mind, and soul. These things have no social graces, they just are. You cannot buy new emotions and you cannot alter your soul. At best, you can convince your mind that you are someone you are not. The problem is, trying to be someone you are not (for any reason) only causes a war between your soul and mind. Eventually, you lose touch with yourself and live a very frustrated, unfulfilling life. I am not suggesting we stop acknowledging obvious moments of appropriate behaviors—like not dropping our pants and pooping in public—but never try to change who you are at the core. This is what makes you YOU, and separates you from every other person in the world. You have something in you that no other human being has, and that the world needs to complete the big picture. Don't withhold that for what only you can see; the picture is so much bigger than the scope of your understanding.

"Riding a horse in not a gentle hobby, to be picked up and laid down like a game of Solitaire. It is a grand passion."

Ralph Waldo Emerson

The Long Way Home

Jr and I took our first long journey together recently. When I say long, it was almost an eight-hour round trip. It was amazing! I learned a lot about Jr that day. Though he is 19 years old, has a little stiffness in his leg, and is typically calm, he has a strength and stamina I didn't give him credit for. There were no

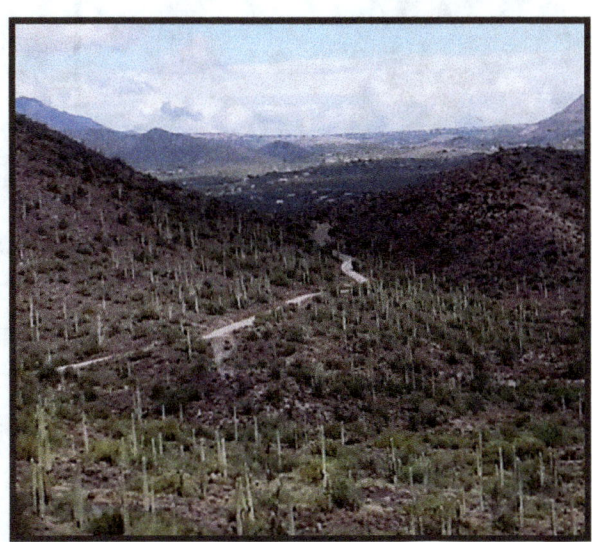

instances of complaining or battles of wills. We rode through some of the most beautiful parts of Arizona to get to our destination and back. On the return trip home, the sun had set and we had to ride through a desert park to get to our street. I couldn't see ten feet in front of me, but thankfully Jr knew the way home. It was perfect synergy between horse and rider for me. I learned how to trust my horse that day because I really had no other option. Riding in the desert in the dark really isn't safe, particularly if you have no idea where you are or how to get to where you are going. Oddly, I felt safe; the choice of liquid for the day didn't hurt, but I had a feeling we'd get home just fine. "They" say horses know the way home, I guess they are right.

A home is so much different than a house. Though I may be thousands of miles from the house I grew up in, I have learned that home is a place you go to in order to feel safe and loved, and where you can shut out the world. Home is wherever my mom is when I have reached the end of myself and just need a place to rest my soul; and that has happened even while we were miles apart. Home is far more than a house and the physical bodies of familiar people. It is that place I find solace, whether it be 2 Hemlock Street, Joliet, IL, or in the middle of the desert on my horse. On this journey called life, we often take the long way home, stumbling through the dark, not entirely sure where we are going. But, when we get there, we know we are home, for the door is always open and we find we were never really that far away to begin with.

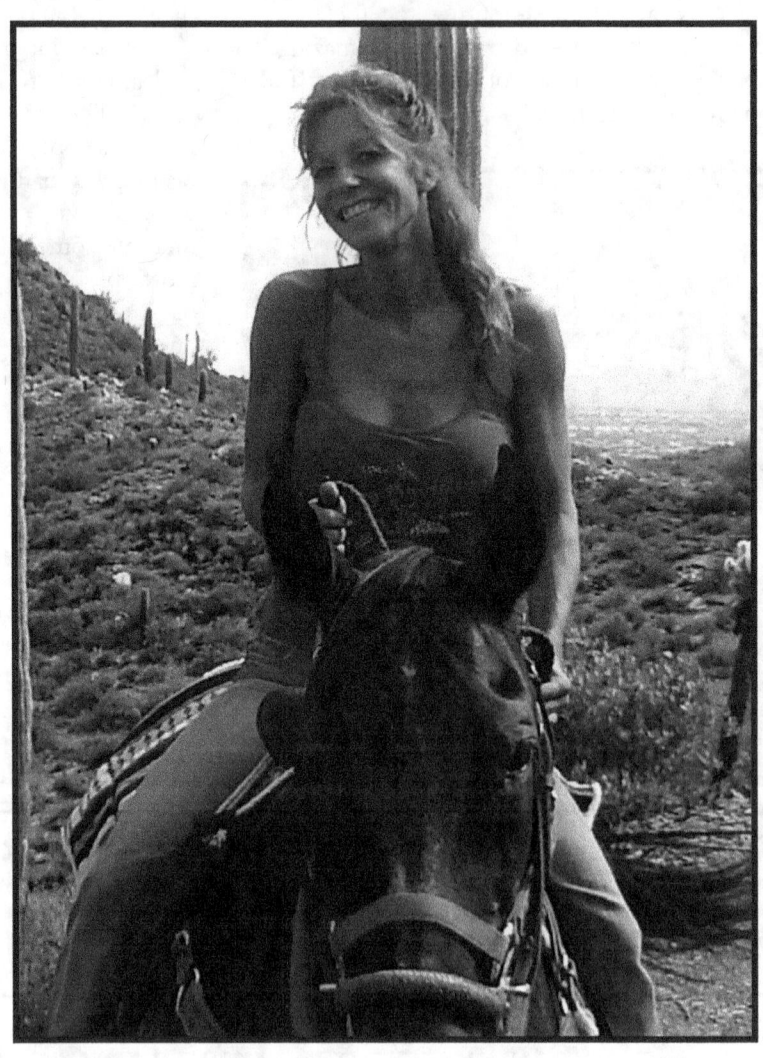

Poker Face

In Harley terms bikers go on a Poker Run, in horse terms it's called a Poker Ride. Unlike two wheels on nicely paved roads with bar stops on your journey, you're on four legs with a few watering holes for your horse, and for you a cooler filled with libations attached to your horse. There are no private bathrooms on a Poker Ride—just a few bushes to hide behind before the group behind you catches up. My first Poker Ride with Jr went great! He was a little jumpy at first when he was among about a hundred unfamiliar horses and people. But once we got a little space between all the riders, he happily followed my lead and we enjoyed about a three-hour adventure through beautiful mountain terrain. The day of riding in and of itself, was uneventful in respects to those silly little scenarios I like to make light of (well, except for the many tiny cactus needles I'm still pulling out of my body from those libation-induced potty breaks).

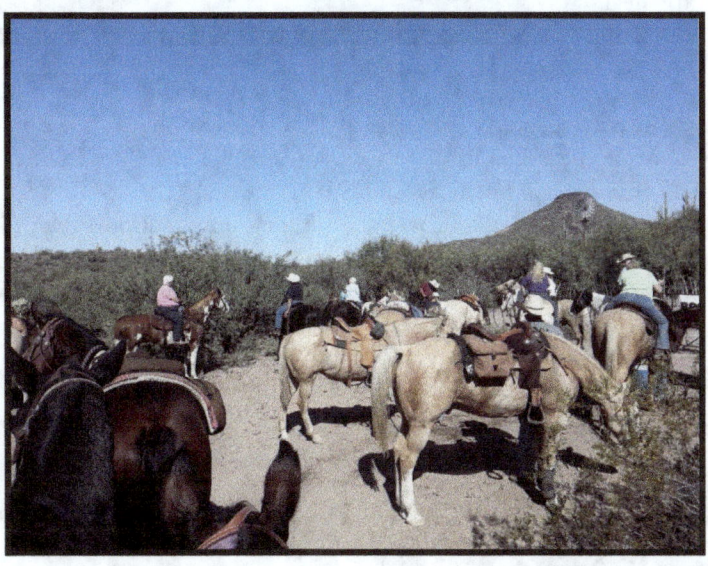

After the ride, we tied our horses to the trailer while my friends and I joined the group for lunch and games. Everything seemed fine when we returned until I tried to lead Jr into the trailer. Jr didn't want to get in. It looked like he had started to limp. We did finally get him in, but when we got home, he was limping terribly. My friends and I couldn't figure out what had happened to Jr to cause him such obvious pain. Of course we attended to his needs, hosed him down, put him in the softest stall, closed off the area to limit his movement, and let him rest. When I returned later to check on him, he was lying down and just looked at me with a "help me" gaze in his eyes. By the next day he was worse. He just lay there all day. A sweet, dear friend who lives next door came by to take a look at Jr. She is very educated about horses, just a notch below a vet.

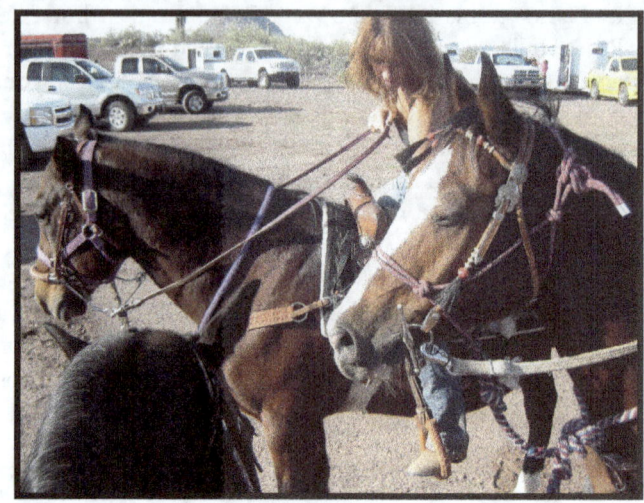

She suspected he had torn a ligament and though it was bad, it didn't appear to be a broken leg. I realized it would take a long time to heal. It had only been eight months since I had a torn ligament and tendon repaired in my leg. Jr patiently waited for me to heal, I could do the same.

Terri and I watched him closely. I sat by him for hours that day and when I left, he was heavily sedated. Terri and I decided we would call the vet in the morning. Despite the initial thought it was a torn ligament, we both feared he actually did break his leg. For horses, this is an inevitable, untimely death. Their bodies are so big and heavy, a broken leg simply cannot support them. I had to consider that this could happen and, needless to say, my heart was broken. The rush of emotions running through my head were innumerable; "How could this be? " Did I do something to hurt him? Did I push him too hard?" Terri tried to reassure me that it wasn't anything I did and that I could ride one of the other horses. In that moment, I didn't feel like I could ever ride another horse; I just wanted my Jr.

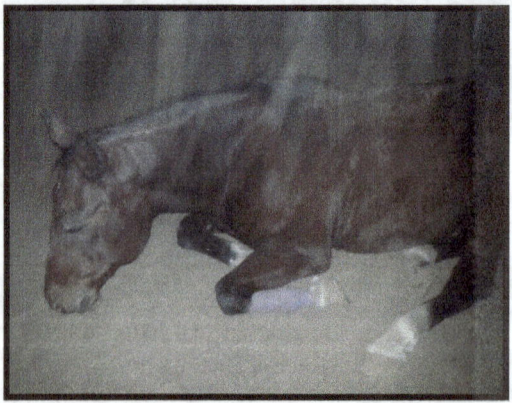

I spent many hours on the ground with him that night and the next day. My heart was breaking. The thought of losing Jr made me sick to my stomach. I've had to endure putting pets down before and it was so hard, but this was infinitely worse. I cannot even articulate how I felt.

Sometimes when pain is so deep, it mentally throws you into a place where simply finding the clarity to just do the next thing takes a mental energy not always readily available. But I have found that hope is a driving force that can move you along. It may be only at a snail's pace, but it is movement nonetheless. We all lose loved ones and feel in that moment we cannot go on, but one thing we must never let go of is hope. Hope in what? Who? For some it is God, for others a dream. For each of us it is something different. But for all of us, the result of hope fulfilled is the same . . . peace in the midst of our madness, joy unspeakable, and a sweet release from the moments that turn our world upside down. Hope . . . we must never lose hope. In this life when we do lose hope, what else do we have?

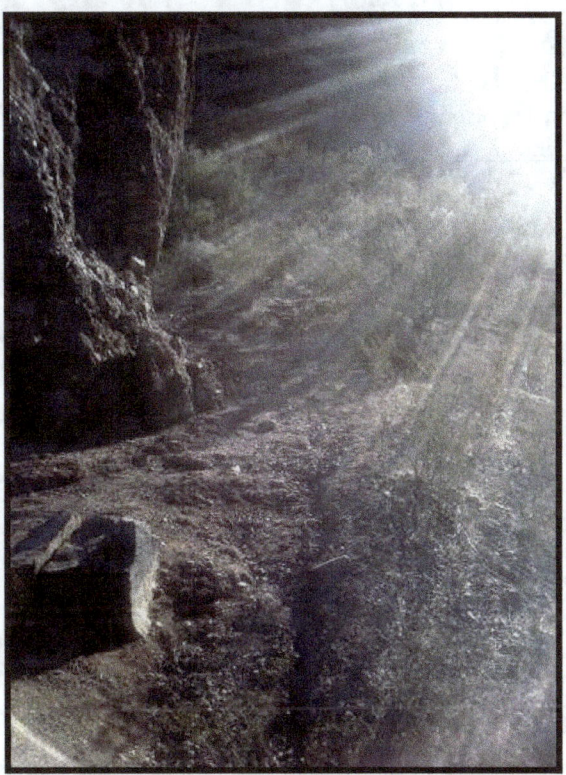

Let the Healing Begin

Thankfully, after it looked as though Jr might have broken his leg, he started to get up and move around a bit. He still hobbled and jumped a little, not putting too much pressure on his leg, but he was up. It was nearly impossible for his leg to be broken. You cannot imagine the joy in my heart to see my boy up and moving, even though the healing road ahead was going to be a long one.

After a few days, there came a point where the pain meds were stopped and he was moved to a smaller stall for his protection. Jr was not happy about this. He had such an attitude problem for a couple of days; he was such a punk! Of course, since he was injured, I still babied him and let him have his moment. That only lasted two days before I finally looked him in the eye and told him to stop it! He just looked at me like "whatever." It was time to let the healing begin and not allow him to milk the situation. I needed to stop babying him and enabling him to be comfortable as the victim. Do horses really do that? Oooh, yes they do.

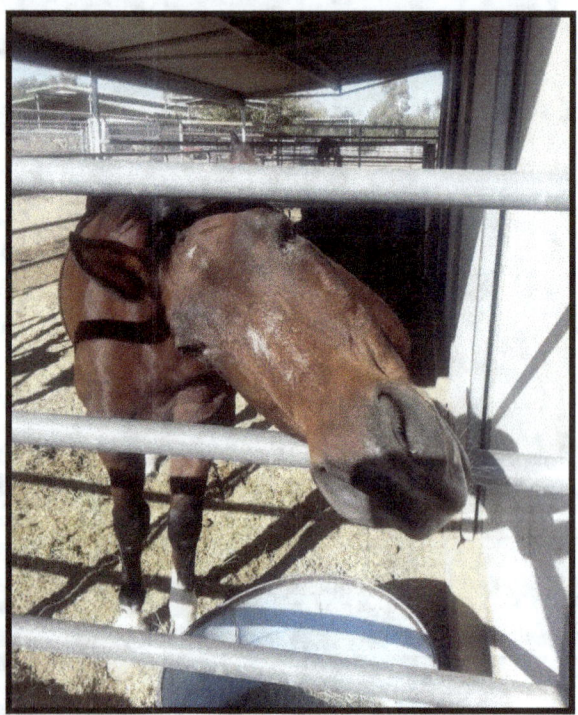

Being the victim is an interesting concept. Everyone feels sorry for the victim, and rightly so. But even true victims of actual misdeeds not brought on by themselves come to a point where they have to stop viewing the world and everyone around them as the enemy. The world is a scary place, but it is where we live. We can move away, run away, hide, or hibernate; but the reality is that the world around us is not going away. We can always find compassionate people to enable our victim mentality, but why? Isn't it far better to overcome barriers, forgive those who have wronged us, and find peace of mind?

Patience My Dear

After Jr hurt himself and began the healing process, patience on my part was vital. I was prepared to wait weeks, even months, to ride him; but I wasn't prepared for his first bath after his injury. The first part of bathing a horse entails getting him in the wash rack. Heretofore, Jr had loved baths, so this part should have been easy. Well, for whatever reason, he just didn't want to get in. I tried all the appropriate measures. I pulled, stood my ground, and even walked him in a small circle, but nothing was working. We just stood there at the foot of the step-up, and he looked at me with apprehension. After a few minutes, I realized that the last thing we did before he was down for a couple of days was bathing. I could almost feel his fear. I talked to him and kept reassuring him it was ok. I put my head down on his level and stood just a few feet in front of him and waited. He took one step closer and put his muzzle by my face. Of course, I kissed him and loved on him. We did this step by step for easily six minutes: I'd take one step back, Jr would, after a minute or two, take another step forward, I'd reward him with kisses and hugs. Then I'd take another step back, and we'd go through the whole cycle again. Six minutes may not seem like a long time, but for something that usually takes a minute or less, it seemed like an hour! Thankfully, bath time was good and Jr was extremely affectionate and happy. Of course, after letting him dry and cleaning up his small stall area with fresh bedding (shavings to make it soft and dry), he rolled.

Though it only took six minutes to get through Jr's apprehension, it felt like a really long time. In retrospect, I learned a very valuable lesson. My patience with this first step in the healing reassured Jr that I was going to see his healing through and not push him beyond his ability. This reinforced the trust between us, which I had feared would be lost during this break from riding. There's a stillness and peace when getting past the first step when it isn't forced. There's a patient assurance in that first and scariest step that once you take it, it's behind you. You can then move forward with confidence no matter what the next step brings.

A Firm Foundation

Jr's stall tends to get a deep divot in the step between his indoor stall and outdoor stall area. Before he came to Terri, he spent a lot of time just standing in a small stall area with little exercise and not-so-soft ground to stand on. He has a little arthritis in his front feet that may be due to this, which may also contribute to the way he enters and leaves his stall. After Terri had a huge pile (10 tons) of dirt delivered, we shoveled and moved dirt for days and days! Talk about hard work! It wasn't as simple as just that. We had to water it down a few times after raking it to make sure it packed down properly. Layer after layer of

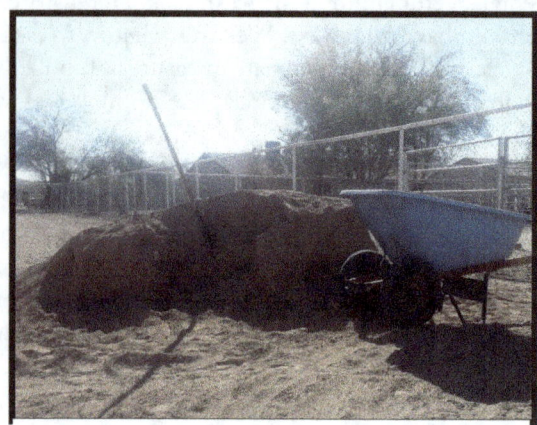

Before

raking and adding dirt and water until it compacted to a level high enough to make the step over and into the stalls optimum. I wasn't sure if it would ever end! Needless to say, as I write this I am very sore, very tired, and ready to turn off the computer and hit the hay!

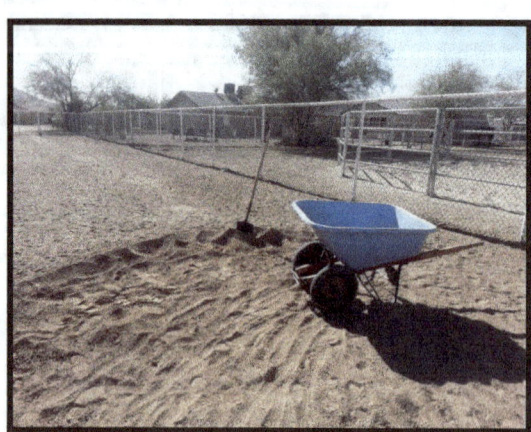

After

All this work was important to build a firm foundation to a stable environment for the horses. It's very important, as their health can be affected by an unstable ground with holes and a near-concrete feeling below them. One web site I read on this topic said if you wouldn't stand on it all day, don't expect your horse to.

A firm foundation makes me ponder the importance of stability. Sometimes we go about life day after day, year after year, and wonder sometimes why things fall apart around us. Is what fell apart built on a firm foundation? Look back to evaluate the building process where it all began. Were you wearing rose-colored glasses back when the foundation was being laid and began building before the foundation settled? You just may have needed a few more loads of dirt and water to firm up the foundation. When a foundation is weak, it caves in under pressure and takes down whatever is on it. If this happens, it's time to take out the shovel and wheelbarrow and start over the right way.

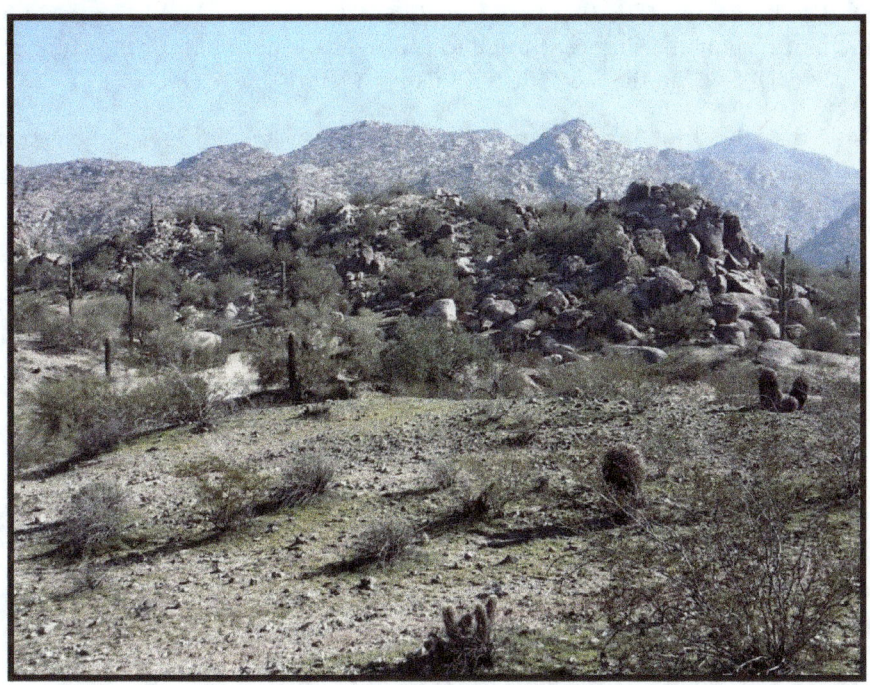

That's Not Mud

The first major monsoon season I endured at the ranch brought more rain in one day than I've seen in a week back in Chicago. The stalls and yard were flooded for days, and chores became very difficult to perform. Feeding was interesting—going stall to stall through the squishy ground. Filling the water buckets, however, was easy. The horses weren't as active as usual, so their water consumption was minimal, and the rain refilled the buckets. The task of shoveling, on the other hand, was quite challenging. Inside the stalls was easy, the piles were identifiable. The outside, however, was an entirely different story. With the heavy rains, there was no way to tell the difference between the mud and the poop! The first time I tried to rake over the mud to help identify the muck below the surface, I came to realize, that's not mud! I made a bigger mess trying to clean the mess, than if I had just left the mess alone.

Isn't that the truth about our best intentions in the midst of the worst situations? We can do our best to make all things right, perfect, and less stressful for all involved, yet find ourselves trying to separate mud from shit. When those two things mix together, they look the same, smell the same and, unfortunately I can tell you from personal experience, they even feel the same. The reality is, sometimes we need to not try so hard to fix what cannot be fixed and simply put down the tools, wash our hands of it, and walk away.

"Closeness, friendship, affection; keeping your own horse means all these things."

Bertrand Leclair

The Green-Eyed Monster

During a brief visit to see Jr, my dog Buddy accompanied me. Buddy, a nub butt (no tail, just a nub) Australian Shepherd, had been rescued a few months prior to this visit. He is a good dog who is very docile and gentle with people, but has anger issues with his own species. There was one situation where Buddy displayed dog aggression toward a pug, and thus began my training with Buddy on how to handle his anger issues. Of course with dogs, it's all about dominance—who is the alpha. Buddy may have lived on the streets and had to prove himself to survive, but he is now in a safe home with an Alpha—me. Training with Buddy had been going great! But I think Buddy learned a lesson from Jr that I simply would not have been able to teach him, at least not on the same level.

During this brief visit, I was lovin' on Jr, just petting and hugging him. Jr was responsive, but curious about Buddy. Prior to Buddy's pug war, he used to roam the ranch; since our training, he stays pretty close to me. Buddy was not feeling the whole Jr and momma thing. He was a little unsettled—crying, sitting close to me, and nudging me to pay attention to him. Jr, on the other hand, wasn't really feeling the whole little-critter-attached-to-mom's-hip thing. Jr stuck his head out through the gate and gave Buddy a not-so-friendly nip that made it clear I am his human!!! Poor Buddy jumped back about ten feet in disbelief! He was definitely not taking on a critter that size, even for me! I had to giggle a little. I love my dog and I love my horse, but Buddy needed to be put 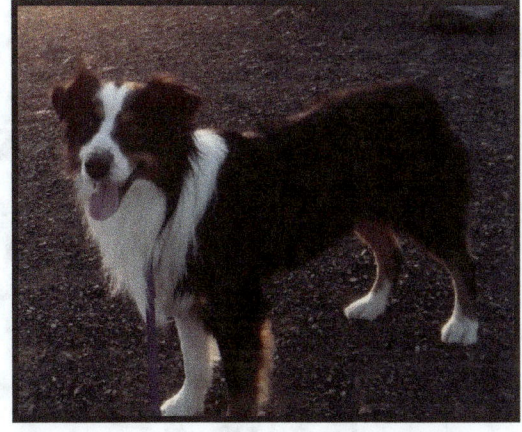 in his place after dominating a dog half his size. Jr made sure Buddy knew his place at the ranch.

This whole scenario was prompted by that green-eyed monster, jealousy. Both my beasts have a loyalty to me that makes each of them very unhappy about my attention and affections going to anyone or anything else. It's really not necessary, but they are animals, so it makes sense. For us humans, dealing with jealousy certainly shouldn't warrant us going up to people and just biting them when we are feeling jealous. Yet, we often do. I have seen and heard more biting words and deeds from people as a result of jealousy, than I have from either of my competitive beasty boys and the rest of their species. (And, yes, I'm including my own sarcastic, defensive behaviors that sometimes sneak in.)

Jealousy, why? It produces nothing good for anyone. It usually involves wanting what someone else has or wanting something from someone who is giving it to someone else. Jealousy is a feeling, and feelings are not wrong. It's what we do with those feelings that sometimes causes irreparable damage. We are not fuzzy, four-footed creatures without human reasoning skills. The next time that green-eyed monster creeps up behind you, be careful not to go biting off people's heads with the sharpness of your words or deeds. Remember, though you may reign as alpha for a minute, there's always someone bigger, smarter, and stronger than you who may have a green-eyed monster just over their shoulder, waiting to bite you back.

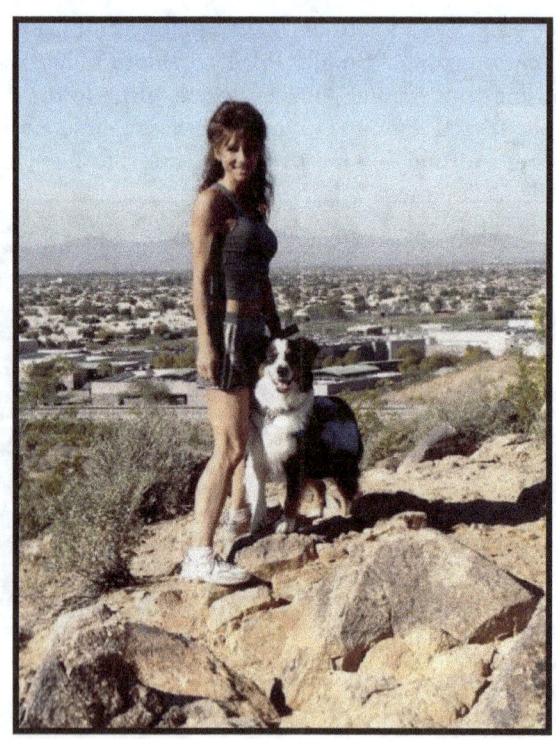

Taking It Down a Notch

Recently I became ill. When I say ill, I actually needed a doctor. I had been in Phoenix three years and still hadn't found a physician until this nasty respiratory infection knocked me out for days! After three days in bed, I'd had enough and just wanted to see my horse. I pulled myself together, got dressed, and drove to the ranch. Oh, how just seeing my baby did me good! We didn't

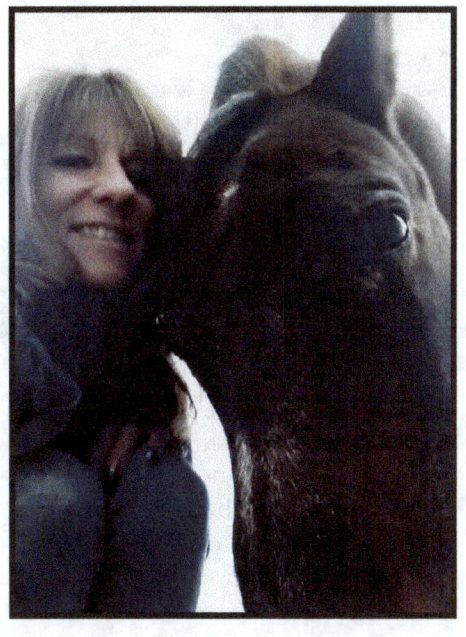

ride, no grooming, no cleaning of stalls; I just reached out to pet my furry friend. He, of course, was receptive, and, to my amazement, sensed I wasn't feeling well. When I stooped down and just watched him head on, he took a few steps forward, stopped in front of me, and put his head gently up against mine. Such a simple moment and sweet horse gesture that was actually quite comforting. It wasn't a big, exciting, funny moment, but an important, much-needed one for me.

Sometimes, the simplest actions can leave the greatest impact on our lives. Too often we are so consumed with our own little worlds that we fail to step close enough toward another's world to gently touch their life. Be it fear, pride, or simply stubbornness, we miss the opportunity to simply show we care. We should never underestimate the power of our words or deeds, be them big or small. They have the power of promoting life or death; they can breathe hope into hopelessness, bring comfort to sadness, and bestow peace in the midst of a storm. Equally as intense, their absence can perpetuate uncertainty, feed discontent, and create a whirlwind of unnecessary anxiety. We are all but human. If we could all just take it down a notch off our high horse, we'd find this life a little easier and a lot more pleasant for all of us.

Pecos Is Done

In my little horse world, I have the pleasure of meeting all kinds of horses. I remember one horse in particular, Pecos, who was as sweet as he was stunning to look at. One of the neighbors from where Jr lives came up the driveway to say hello, and I was captivated by Pecos as he approached me. Pecos was a loving horse; he put his muzzle out to me as if he wanted to be kissed, so, of course, I obliged. Pecos' human said he loves kisses and, based on his reaction, I could tell it was definitely true.

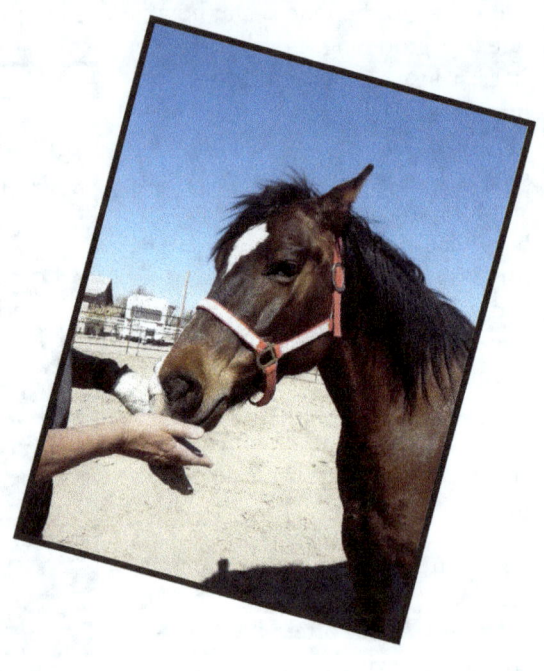

As we talked, I commented on how beautiful his coloring was. His overall color was almost a dark golden brown, with a slightly deep red hue to it. He had white socks that were met with black that ran up his leg and faded out halfway towards his body. He was clothed with a black mane and tail and was simply stunning.

Pecos' human said to me "Pecos is done." I just looked at him with sadness and concern. "He's done?" I asked. "Yes, Pecos is done, D.U.N., dun," he replied.

I know I must have had the most confused look on my face as I wondered if that was cowboy for "done," and grieved for the poor animal's fate. It wasn't long into that conversation, however, that it was explained to me that "dun" is a horse coloring. I could only laugh at the reminder of just how much of a novice I still am in the horse world.

This colorful little conversation also reminds me of a principle I have tried to pattern my words after: "Say what you mean. Mean what you say." Sometimes, communicating what we mean to say isn't always easy. It's so easy to

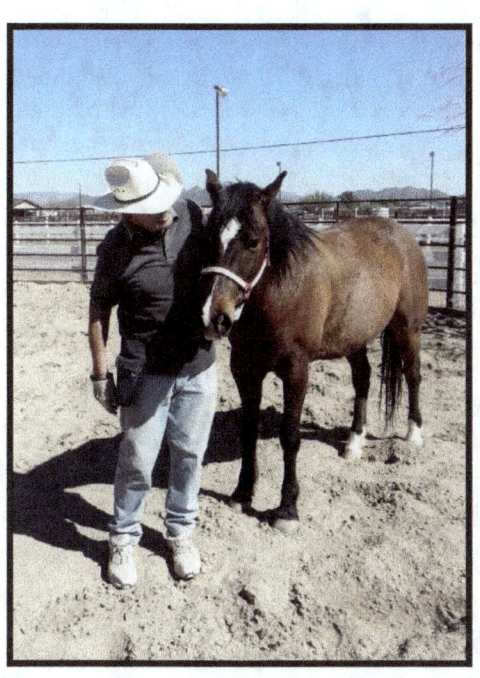

misunderstand words, especially when you add body language, patterns of behavior, or, given today's technology, texts that remove all other factors (including actual words that might make the meaning clearer). To say that Pecos was done, or dun in this case, communicated information about his coloring only if the hearer understood that meaning of dun. However, to say that to a somewhat uneducated horse owner/rider articulated that Pecos' time on earth was short. Humorous as it was, those words made me sad, even if just for a few moments. The clarity brought by defining the difference between "done" and "dun" eased my mind considerably. No harm done. Yet, how often do we assume our words (or lack thereof) don't cause unnecessary negative emotions to those we speak (or don't speak) them to?

Be very careful what you say and sure of what you mean, but don't stop there. Be certain that the one who hears you is clear about what they heard. By doing so, you may save someone undue stress caused by misunderstanding. You may also save a relationship.

Hello??? Are Ya with Me???

One rainy evening in horse world, I went to feed the gang. Of course, as I walked into the barn, Jr quickly came to his stall door to greet me. He was a little agitated, probably because of the rain and the added fact it was feed time. He gave a quick hello, good to see you, now feed me moment of his time; when I say moment, that would be about 3.4 seconds. Obviously, he was hungry and figured he should be nice to the hand that feeds him, but he made it clear by the way he looked at me, then put his face in his feed bin, then looked back at me repeatedly that he was past the "I've missed you!" moment and quickly advanced to "Feed me already!" After feeding everyone, I went to say goodbye to my furry friend. Typically, even at feed time, I get some kind of a response—a head raised, muzzle rub, something…not this time. I stood by the stall door, scratched his neck, and talked to him. He didn't so much as turn his gaze away from his food. All I could hear was the rustling of pellets and chomping of his food. Really?? I drag my butt out of my warm home to trample through the mud and feed you in the rain, and you can't even lift an eyelid to look at me! Punk! Yeah…punk.

It is actually funny; Jr is a horse who behaves more like a pig at feed time. I don't expect him to understand the effort it took me to slosh around in the rain. It would be silly to think he even could.

However, as human beings with at least some reasoning ability, we all too often take people for granted. Whether we become so engrossed in our own issues or let something else take priority over them in that moment, we are delusional if we think they do not see or feel it. When we fail to recognize other's efforts to impress upon our world whatever it is they are giving—time, conversation that lets you into who they are, and even monetary blessings—we leave an impression with that person that they are unimportant and not worth our time or attention. That doesn't sound very nice does it? Yet, we do it. We all do it and, typically, we do it to those we say we love the most. The most unfortunate thing is that, in our selective ignorance, we create a great chasm. After time, we push people who were once so close, very far away and unreachable.

Wow, a simple little act of reminding someone they matter to you by treating them with the respect of your time and uninterrupted attention could make the biggest difference between those who go and those who stay in your life. Now, if you don't want them in your life but you lack the internal fortitude to tell them that, keep taking them for granted and it won't be long before that is no longer an issue.

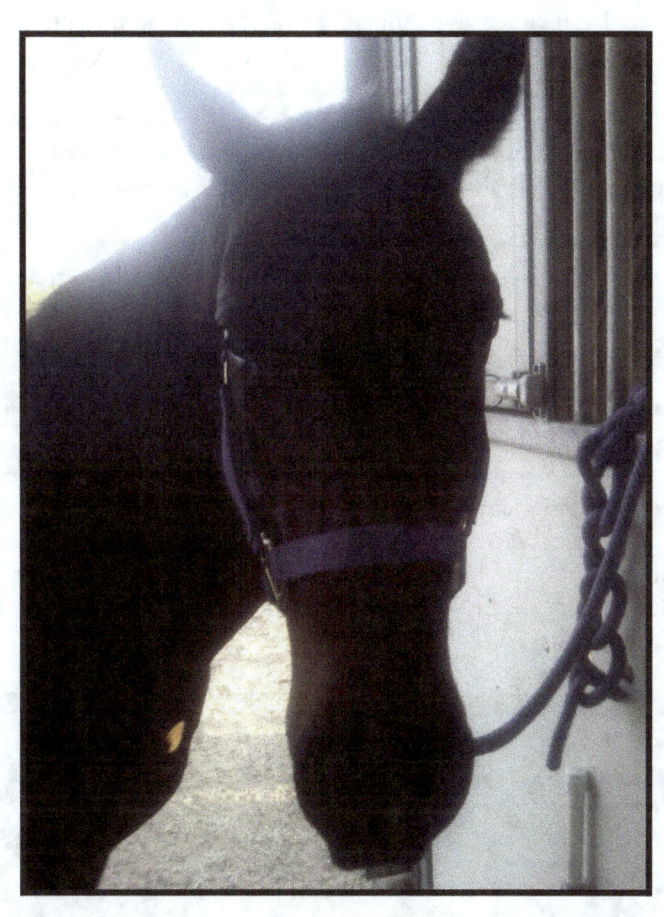

Destined to Fail

There are days when Jr displays behaviors that indicate he is just not up for venturing out into the world. Sometimes he can be lackadaisical about everything from grooming to saddling up and hitting the trail. Sometimes he's a li'l cranky and purses his lips and throws back his ears. In those moments, I have a choice. I can either give him a break and just let him pout, or I can hop up in the saddle and ride out his mixed emotions. I have found riding it out is typically not a whole lot of fun for either one of us. We engage in our horse-to-human debates, and, though I inevitably win, it just isn't a very satisfying victory. In the same manner, when I've let him have his moment and just kind of step back, Jr has walked up next to me and changed his composure, resulting in a great ride!

Isn't that true about our human relationships as well? It's a tireless struggle trying to convince someone to be something they are not just to satisfy your need, or trying to prevent them from being or doing what satisfies their need. Any time you have to engage in preventative measures that alter a person's desires or wishes from being fulfilled, you are destined to fail. You lose the joy of choice and the discovery of compromise. In all relationships, there should be a give and take that meets somewhere in the middle. Otherwise, you foolishly create resentment, tension, and a faulty foundation to build on. Just as with Jr, sometimes it is best to just step back and let the other person figure out what they want more in that moment. If it's to ride on together, you meet in the middle, and it will be so much more enjoyable for both of you. If not, is it really worth fighting for failure?

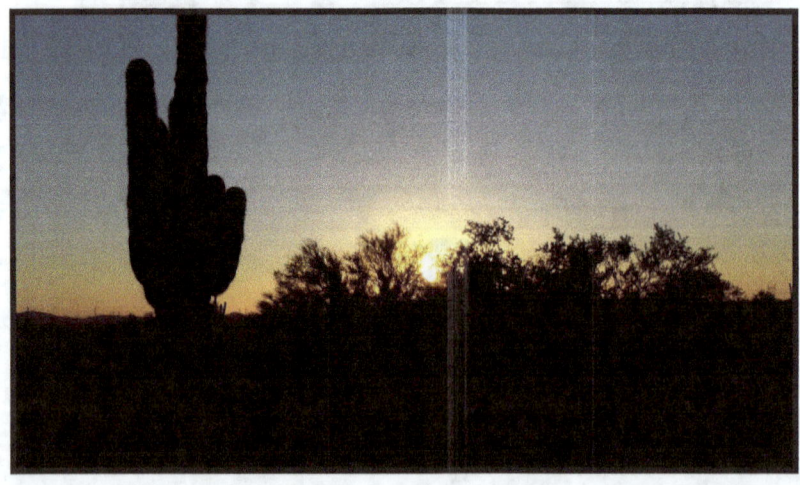

In the Trenches

The morning after a heavy rainfall, the stables were a sloshy, flooded mess. Poor George was several inches under water, making it not only messy, but a health risk to his hooves. Bright and early, Terri and I were sloshing around, digging trenches to release the floodwaters from his stall and direct them to the street. Sounds easy enough, right? Grab a shovel and dig. Alas, no task is ever as easy as it sounds.

This easy little trench-digging party entailed climbing a 10-foot fence, which I got hung on before reaching the other side. When I finally began digging in, I had to be *very* careful not to fall, as my footing was completely unstable due to the muddy mess I was digging through. I almost took an unplanned, early-morning muck bath a few times. It didn't take long, but the rigorousness of it all left both Terri and me out of breath, reminding us that we're not the spring chickens we once were. The result of our efforts produced a steadily flowing stream of horse urine, poop, and rainwater that found its way to the street. Not sure how the neighbors felt about that, but George appeared to appreciate it.

Digging trenches is an interesting task. If they are not an even depth all the way through, the water gets stuck and even reverses its flow backwards. I saw this a few times when I didn't dig deep enough in certain parts of the trench. There was one point where the ground was so hard it was impossible to make it even. The only solution was to dig deeper, which meant the ground after that had to be just as deep. It worked, but it sure wasn't as simple as dig it and go. We had to test the water flow and watch it. When all the water kept flowing where we wanted it to go, we cleaned off our shovels and called it a day.

Digging deeper. Isn't it amazing how the rush of life's misfortune can flood us with a desire to just give up? We can know where we want our water to flow. Yet, if we don't pay attention and dig deeper where we need to, the stream reverses its direction and we find ourselves back where we started. Is it worth all the mental energy, inconvenience, and time you need to invest? Guess that depends on whether your investment genuinely accomplishes the goal or is simply something to do in the moment for a temporary fix.

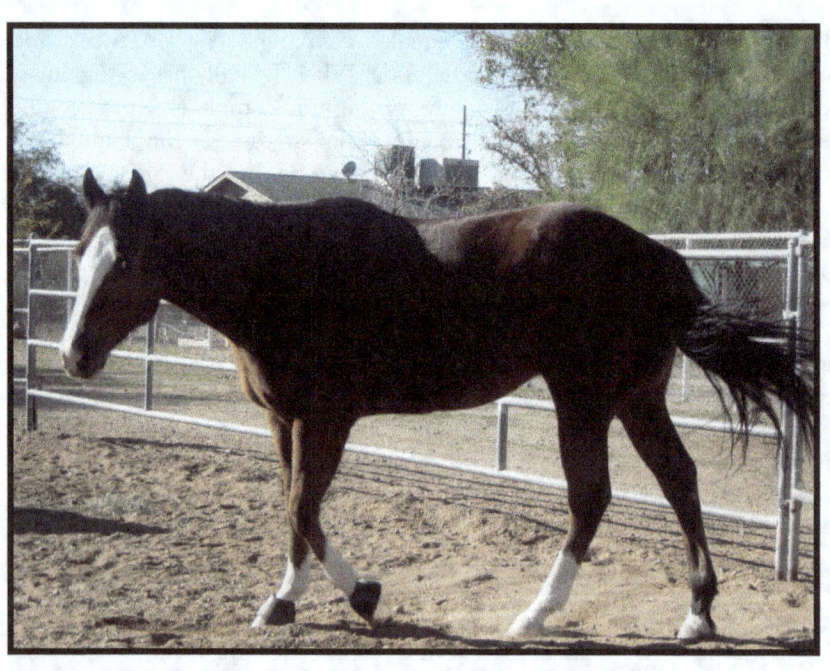

Backed into a Corner

Terri is a cute little country girl. She stands all of 5'2" (and ¼ inches). She typically uses a barrel to get up on her horse, not for a lack of flexibility or strength but just to make the task easier. Leroy is a big boy; silly, full of energy, and fun to play with. When you put these two in the arena for a workout, it is just plain ol' fun to watch. Leroy runs his circles on command like he should

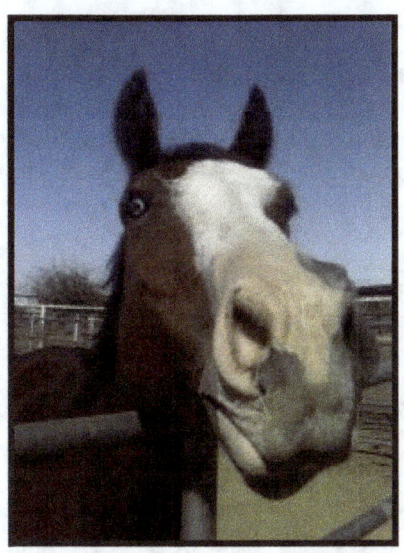

but, sometimes, he just doesn't want to stop. Of course, Terri will get him running harder and faster for a bit. But when it is time to stop and she means it, these two may look like they are playing, but boy does she get angry! One day, she had him cornered on one end of the arena, he didn't actually stop completely, and he sort of paced to the left, then to the right. He would get all wound up, and Terri would stomp her feet, moving towards him with every shift in his direction. This little thing was going head to head with the jolly Leroy giant! It was amazing to see. She got him stopped, but not for long. Round and round the arena he went again, until she tried to stop him and the "make me stop game" began again. Finally, Leroy stopped and succumbed to the realization that Terri was not giving up, and if he wanted to be rewarded, he needed to just chill out and let her lead. Game over. Terri was tired, Leroy was happy, and it turned out to be a really good day after that little display of good sportsmanship.

Being backed into a corner just doesn't feel good for anyone. For a horse, it is necessary to train them and bring into control the animal behavior that could be harmful if not tamed. As humans, it is unnecessary; imposing your will on another only creates resentment and discontent, leaving a person feeling trapped. To try and make someone do something they really don't want to do removes their free will, which pretty much removes the joy for all involved. I've learned it is best to express your feelings, and then allow people to do what they want. If they want you to be a part of it, great! If not, then what is the point? Sure, there are many ways to back people into a corner, but do you really want to engage in anything with someone who really doesn't want to be there?

Shit and Shavings

There it was one day, bigger than life in a huge pile in the middle of the arena. Terri had ordered a huge truckload of wood shavings to be put in the horse's stalls (34 yards). It looked soft, smelled good, and screamed, "Time to get out the wheelbarrow and shovel again!" Though relocating shavings is nowhere near the task of shoveling dirt, it is still hours of back and forth, to and from each stall.

Of course, I had researched the benefits and found shavings in a horse's stalls provide many benefits—more warmth, drier stalls, less dust, and, most interesting to me, the additional softness can provide a better, deeper sleep for your horse. Much like humans, when a horse goes into a deeper sleep, he relaxes all of his muscles if he sleeps lying down, and shavings are believed to offer a more inviting place to lie down.

Contrary to popular belief, however, my personal experience has shown that shoveling shit out of shavings is *not* easier. Maybe the fear of disposing of the costly shavings with the waste makes you a little more careful when sorting between the two!

A good night's sleep as it relates to sorting through a valuable, positive substance and a load of crap, though humorous in the horse world, challenges the laugh reflex in my reality. I highly doubt I am the only person who has experienced broken sleep (as a horse does when he's trying to sleep standing up). For a horse, a soft inviting place to lie down can solve the problem. For a human mind, however, sorting through a load of crap isn't quite as easy as seeing the big chunks and mucking them out.

How does one actually put away the muck-chucking tool when lying down for the day? I guess, like a horse, you just sleep on it. Yes, horses do that, disgusting as that sounds and smells. Until it is cleaned up for them, there is just no other way it will be removed. So, being the smart creatures they are, they just sleep on it. And wouldn't ya know, it's still there when they wake up! Why, then, can my brain not grasp that concept? Some things you just cannot sort through. You just need to sleep on it, get the rest you need, and sort through with a fresh perspective in the morning.

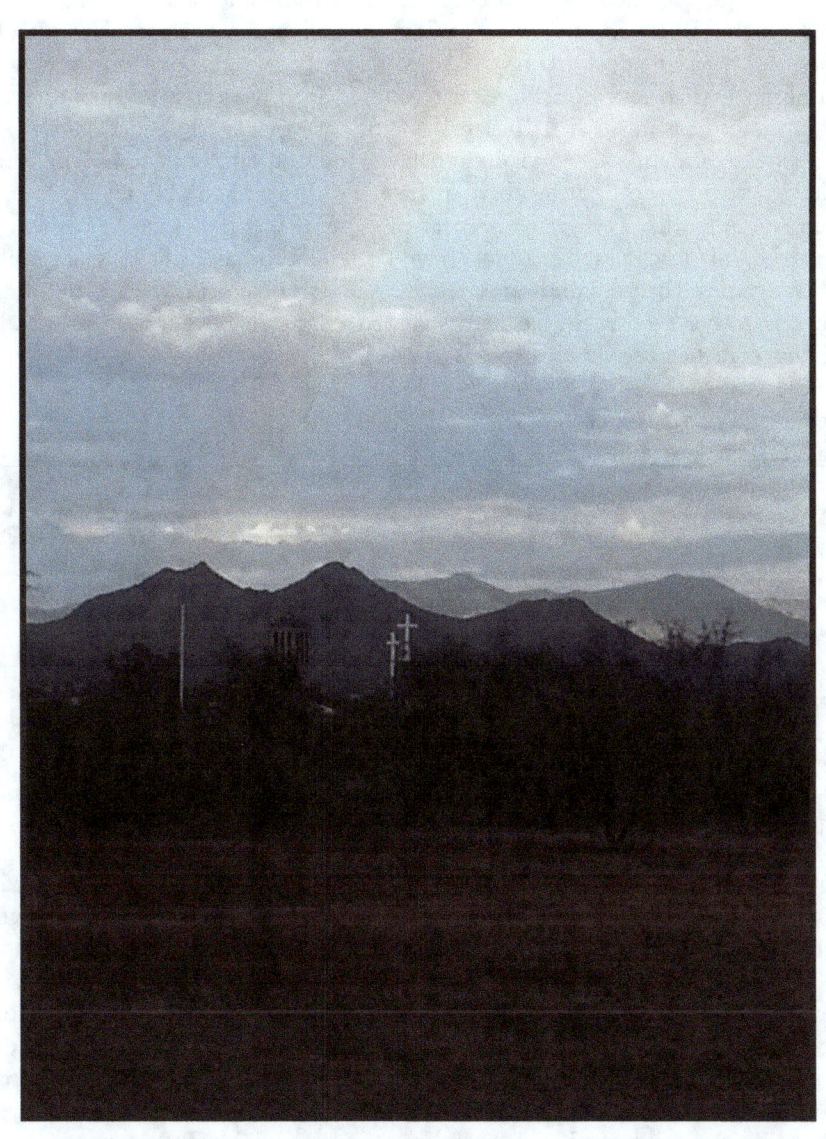

Insanity

One trail ride with Terri and a friend, Christy, I learned a lot as my teacher was being taught. Terri rode Filly, Christy was on Cali, and I of course was joyfully riding Jr. Jr was an angel that day. No resistance to my directions, no wanting to run home, just an easy ride. Filly, on the other hand, was all hyped up. She just didn't want to listen to Terri! Christy, being full of experience, offered Terri some good advice. She told Terri to lightly snap the reins on one side and pull Filly in a little. She said not to do it too hard at first, but that if she didn't respond, do it again a little harder. Terri was to repeat this and, if that didn't work, she was to then take Filly in circles. Terri must have done this routine with Filly ten times. As I hung in the back a little and watched, Filly started to act up again but, oddly, Filly turned her head in before Terri snapped the reins. Terri asked Christy why she did that; her answer made sense.

Christy explained that Filly now knows what to expect when she behaves that way; she was expecting Terri to snap the reins.

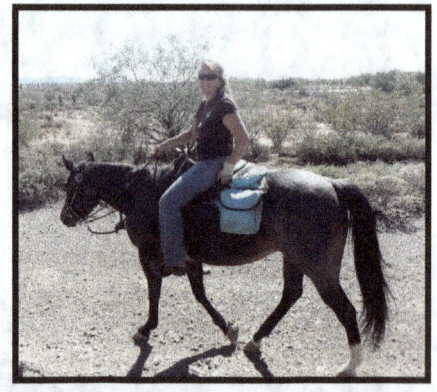

Insanity is widely defined as doing the same thing over and over and expecting a different result. Isn't that the truth? So often we wonder why nothing changes when we do not change our behavior. I found it interesting that Filly quickly grasped the concept of how her repeated behavior would get the same repeated response. In fact, she understood this so well that she reacted to the expected response before Terri even did it.

Now of course, we can look at this and rightfully think of how we repeatedly do the same thing over and over and think it will end up differently. However, being the observer in this, I came to realize as the rider, the one in control of me, I need to be smarter about foreseeing the result of repeated behavior. With horses you can actually feel a change in them before they act up. They may pin their ears back, their breathing pattern may change; even a little twitch under their saddle can indicate a change of behavior. Likewise in life, if you pay attention, you will see repeated behaviors producing repeated results, even before they're evident. If we tune in to what outside influence causes a repeated reaction from us and make a change in our response at the first indicator, before the pattern begins, we just might see a different result. Otherwise, it's simply just insanity.

Where There's a Will, There's a Way

After the task of moving the shavings from the arena into the stalls, there were still several large piles of shavings throughout the area. You'd think it would be easy to spread it around the arena to make the ground flat so there are no stumbling blocks for the horses. Well, as I found in my attempt to spread the shavings, doing so is not as simple as it looked. Although shavings are relatively light, when compacted together they are actually quite heavy. Kicking the piles and raking them was actually not so easy to do. After taking Jr in the arena to help me, we quickly decided not to try that route. Jr was tripping over the piles and, after his accident, it just wasn't wise to have him in there. We didn't have a tractor, either. So, after putting Jr in his stall, I realized I needed to pull out the rake and get busy.

About that time, however, a friend pulled up to the stall with his pick-up truck and drove around to the arena. He hooked a piece of chain-link fence to his truck and attached two heavy boards to it with a chain. He pulled into the arena and drove around in circles for at least 40 minutes. He looked like a little kid happily playing in a ball pen at McDonalds. Tractor? We didn't need no stinkin' tractor! We all wanted the arena to be prepared for the horses and where there's a will, there's a way!

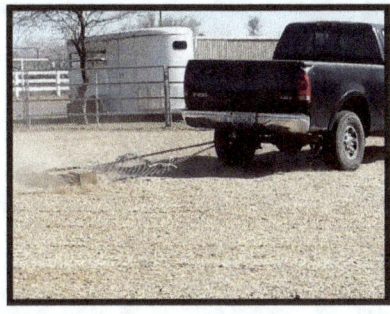 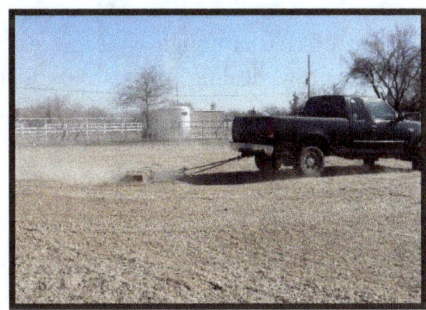

Where there's a will, there's a way. We hear that said often, but I don't think the way is ever truly the problem. We all want something, that part is indisputable. But I have found that if you want something bad enough, we humans inevitably find a way to have it. Be it something big, small, or seemingly insignificant; be it for ourselves or someone we love. If we truly want it, we manage to make it happen.

Really think about that—is it a matter of figuring out how to get what you want or is it simply just knowing what you want? I would have to guess, if you are anything like me, the hardest part is being sure of what you want. Getting it, though it may take sacrifice and work on your part, is actually the easier part.

Live and Let Go

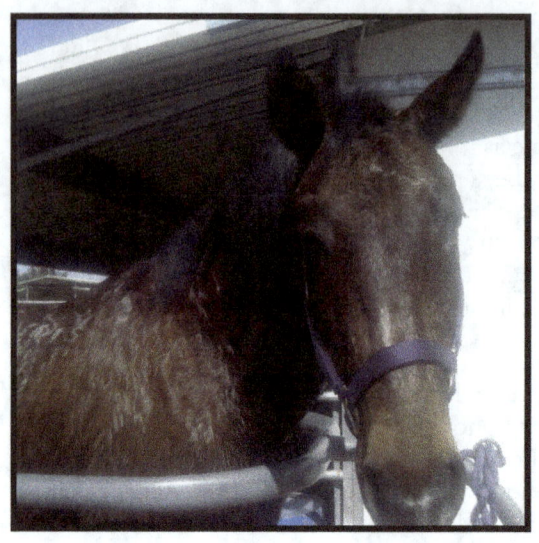

Since Jr's injury, it has been a process of physically rehabilitating him. He seemed to be doing fine on our short rides until recently, but now he has developed a real problem with tripping. At first we couldn't figure out the reason, but have now deduced that his age and lack of activity during the past few months have contributed to sore joints. Although he had had some issues with tripping in the past, I had hoped they were worked out. Apparently, that part of him was not truly healed, but will always be a sore spot for him.

I've realized that although we can mask the pain with medication and naturally try to promote healing, my baby is just older and war torn. The unfortunate, inevitable reality is that he is closer to retirement than I want to admit. How it pains me to even type that! My eyes are welling up with tears and my stomach is turning. Thankfully, that doesn't mean he needs to be put down, just that riding him rigorously could be painful for him and risks an injury due to an imbalanced stride when we ride.

Though Jr's riding days are by no means over, the extent to which we can ride is limited. It's heartbreaking, as there is a part of me that just can't let go of the thought that he's MY horse and I just want to ride MY horse. We connect, we flow, and we have fun together. I continue to hope his health will just miraculously change, but the reality is, it won't.

Sometimes, no matter how badly you want something to change, or how deeply you hope, some things just will not change, or at least not in the way you'd hope they would. There have been moments when Jr appears better and we can happily resume life as horse and rider, but, unfortunately, without age reversal or a miracle drug, things must change for me and Jr. If I unintentionally push him too hard, it could actually cause him real harm.

Letting go of an idea or habit is hard, even if it isn't a healthy one. Although I will continue to work with Jr and try to restore his strength, I'm having to face a new reality. His old age and years of work followed by a sedentary life make me realize I must let go of the expectations and hopes I have had for many years of carefree riding adventures together. Letting go will require me to open myself up to the idea of not just riding another horse, but investing in the connection and bond that must be forged to create trust. Trust is important, though scary at times. Trust entails putting yourself out there with the knowledge you could get hurt, but it also provides opportunities to find the things in life that only dwell on the other side of that trust. To live, you must let go . . . of the past, of the ideals, of the habits. Otherwise, you're not really living, just re-living that which you cling to.

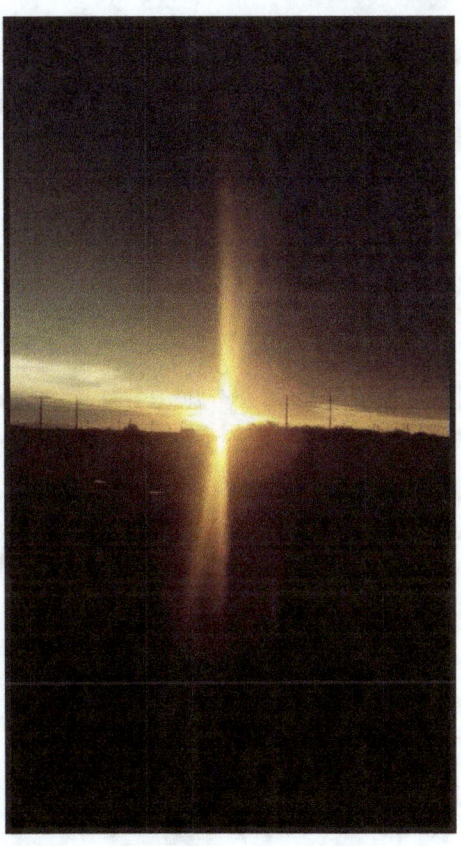

A Horse Among Cows

One spring evening, Terri and I took a sunset ride through our favorite desert park. About two weeks before, we had noticed that the entrance had a gate that wasn't there before. We didn't really know why it was there. We just opened the gate, closed it behind us and rode, and then repeated this action when we returned.

Jr was feeling better. We had found out he had an abscess in his frog and the farrier (horseshoe guy) took care of this. Now that he was not in pain riding, he was full of piss and vigor (as my mom would call it). He was feeling so good our entire ride that he did the "Happy Trot." The Happy Trot is a pace somewhere between a walk and fast trot, typically done on the way home after you reach the halfway point in a long ride. It probably looks a little silly, like a horse running in place. But it's actually pretty fun to feel your horse move with somewhat of a happy spring in his step.

Our ride was unusual for us; we took the path in but decided just to wander through the desert landscape off the trail on the way back. We had no real idea where we were, but we knew how to find our way back when the sun started setting. A friend of mine had been drilling into my mind the concept of using the sun as my compass for both riding and driving. It has actually been working out for me!

After an hour or so we got back on a trail heading home, when we encountered a herd of cows. It was very odd to see these marked beasts out in the field. Suddenly the whole gated park thing made much more sense. Terri and I were a little unsure how our horses were going to respond to this large group of big black cows, but we really had no other option but to go through them. We were fenced in on the south, the cows extended from the path where we were and far out towards the northeast, and we needed to go east (are you impressed with my use of north, south, and east?). It looked as though going through the herd was inevitable, so we started towards them cautiously. Cali was a little unsure but behaved really good! Jr, to my surprise, stopped the Happy Trot and calmed down. He was so confident and calm, I was amazed. This horse of mine never ceases to amaze me. The way he jumps and freaks out over the smallest of creatures, I had anticipated we would run through this herd and not casually walk by as though we owned the park. After we got past the herd, Cali let out a loud sigh through her nostrils as if to say "Yeah, we are here, we came, we saw, we conquered....(pfffft)."

"A horse among cows." "A fish out of water." "One of these things is not like the other." I imagine we've all felt this way at one time or another. I know I have felt it more than once. It could be due to a new job with all new coworkers, going to a party where you don't know anyone except the person who invited you, or walking through a crowd of people nothing like you; there are many scenarios. How do you handle those moments? As I rode Jr and observed his calm, cool demeanor, I was impressed with his quiet confidence. He didn't need to do anything.

When humans are in a situation like that, I have observed some interesting behaviors. Some people find it impossible not to talk and then typically about themselves; they share stories (made up or true) to promote themselves. Some people behave in a way they normally wouldn't just to fit in. Some people pull into themselves and become very quiet, shy, and introverted. I like Jr's approach. He simply went about his business of getting us to the other side of those cows. He simply put one foot in front of the other, and moved forward naturally, not rushed or cautiously. Next time you are faced with that awkward feeling like being a horse among cows, there is no need to hesitate or panic. Just keep your head held high, the pace steady, and move along.

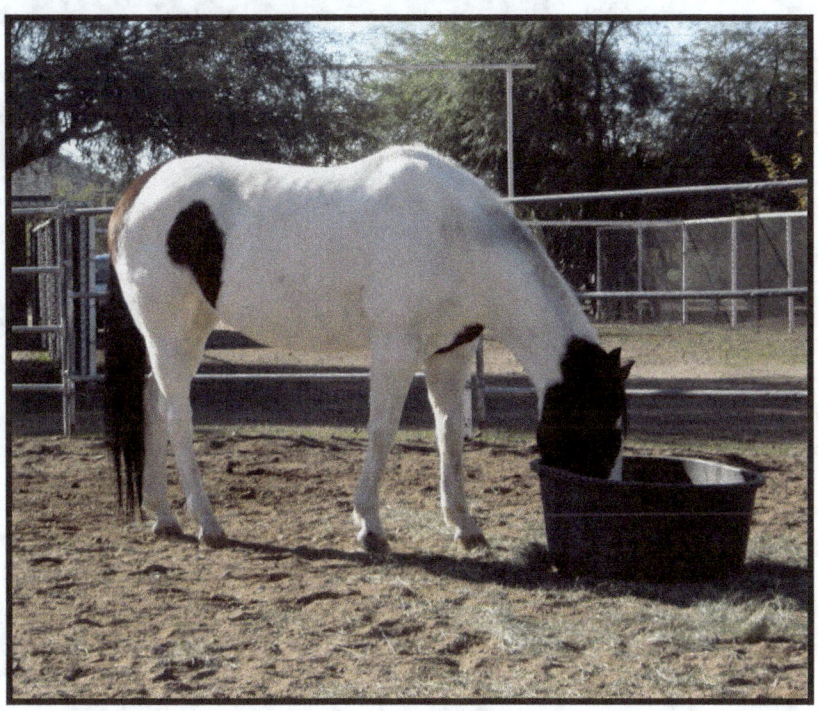

You're Going the Wrong Way!

After a long business trip to the cold state of Ohio, I returned and quickly went to see Jr. Oh how I had missed him! We spent a few hours together just playing, grooming, and taking a little ride. Jr was very well behaved until we came to some construction cones. I didn't push him too hard to deal with those; we just went around them. On the way back to the house, I was a little jet-lagged and spacey. We just kept riding, but suddenly I felt lost. I didn't recognize anything. I didn't actually jump physically, but internally I panicked. Jr, of course, felt it and got a little jumpy. He wanted to turn around but I wasn't ready to because I wasn't altogether sure where I was. It then occurred to me that horses do know the way home. So, I turned him around and, lo and behold, I had passed up our street! I just laughed at myself, patted Jr on the neck and let him take me home.

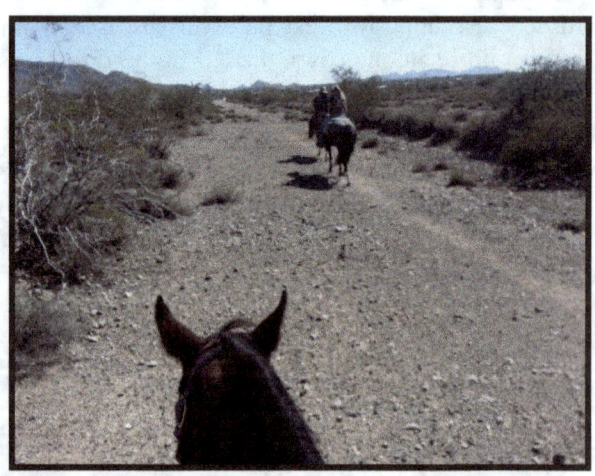

Since Jr and I had our turning point moment, he has been wonderful! Even with my directionally challenged moment, he followed my lead. He knew the way home, but he complied with my directions. I am not suggesting he should have disobeyed my commands—God knows I do not want to deal with that attitude anymore! However, it got me thinking about being led in the wrong direction by those we love and trust. How often do we go along with other's plans for the sake of avoiding confrontation?

Sometimes it's not such a good idea to just wing it and go with the flow. Sometimes we need to be a little bolder and more confident about the direction we want to go. It's not always easy to walk in a different direction than those you love, but sometimes it is necessary to buck up, dig your heals in, and just move forward in the direction you must go to get to your goal.

You Can Lead a Human to Water

Jr can be so direct sometimes it's scary. One day when I arrived, he was in the arena. As usual, he came to greet me with his heartwarming, I'm-so-happy-to-see-you, fast-paced walk as I approached the fence. I, of course, greeted him with a hug and lots of lovin' rubs. That lasted all of about 30 seconds before he quickly started walking away. I followed him as it appeared that's what he wanted me to do. Suddenly, he stopped and put his head into a water bucket, took it out, and looked back at me until I got near the bucket. He put his head back in the bucket, kept his eyes on me, and just stared at me. The bucket was empty and, despite the full bucket of water three feet away, he was letting me know he wanted fresh water in that bucket . . . now. Amazing animals those furry, four-footed friends . . . who said horses can't talk?

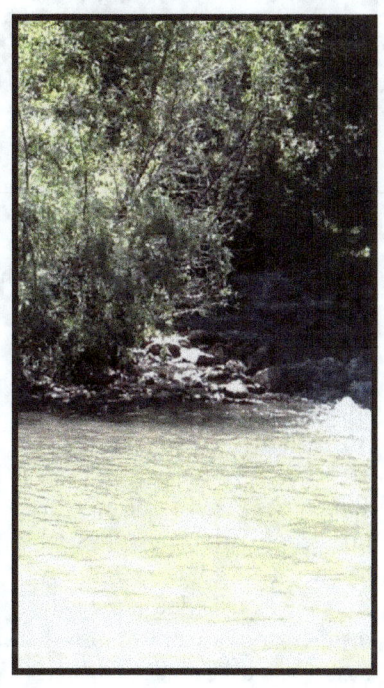

As humorous as that scenario was, it reminded me of an area of patience I have been working on for quite some time. One of the things about humans that really irritates me is when people simply cannot say what they want. I've always had a hard time when adults use the excuse that they don't know what they want. I'm not talking about what to eat for dinner or where to hang out when you meet up with friends. I'm talking about situations where they bitch and moan about their life, do nothing to change it, but when asked what they want, they say, "I dunno." I am inclined to believe they do know but, for whatever reason, can't have it. Yes, I am still a work-in-progress with the whole patience thing. Despite being an overly analytical person, I believe that sometimes people make things way too complicated. Discontentment, stress, and an all-out lack of peace in your soul are pretty good examples of what nobody wants, so why then is it so doggone hard to figure out what you do want? Geesh, if a horse can lead a human to water, or a lack thereof, why do people have such a hard time with matters in life that really matter?

Spineless

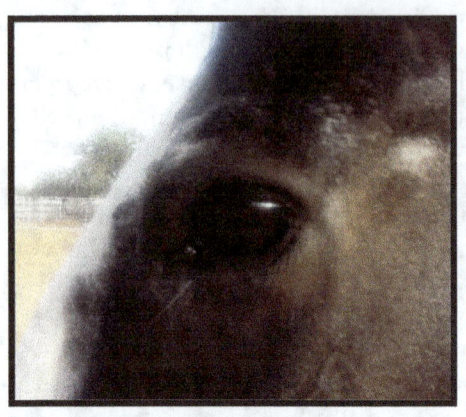

Recently we added a new family member. His name is Black Cloud, Cloud for short. He is just a little younger than Jr, with a mix of brown and black and a big white "cloud" on his face. He was somewhat of a rescue (from a friend of a friend who could no longer care for him). He was in need of some TLC, good nutrition, and exercise. Over the course of a few months, he has come a long way, with one exception, his tail. Poor thing only has half a tail! We've tried everything from nutrition to regular brushing, but the dang thing just won't grow!

Now a horse's tail may not seem to like a big deal unless you are a competitor in shows where the length and health of the tail matters, but there are actual uses for that tail. A lot of those uses are signs to humans and other horses. For example, if a tail is held high, it typically signals good spirits. A tucked-in tail sometimes is a means of protection when a physical exam is going on. A shortened tail doesn't really disturb too many of these uses, as it is clear which direction the tail is going even without the long "skirt" (that pretty part of the tail that extends from the "dock" [muscle and skin covering the tailbone]).

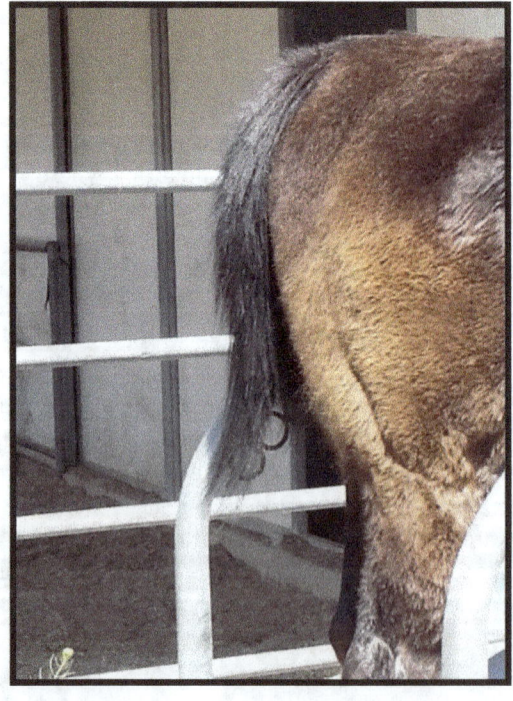

However, it is now fly season and they are out with a vengeance this year! Poor Cloud with his little nubby tail has no defense against these little pests. It may not seem like a big deal to us, but imagine a fly buzzing around you and landing right on your forehead and you have no way to shoo it away. How incredibly irritating! Now let's take it a step further. I have seen horses use their tails to swat people and other horses. Yes, it has happened a time or two when I've been grooming or cleaning a hoof and bam! I've gotten the tail in the face. Humorous, but shocking nonetheless!

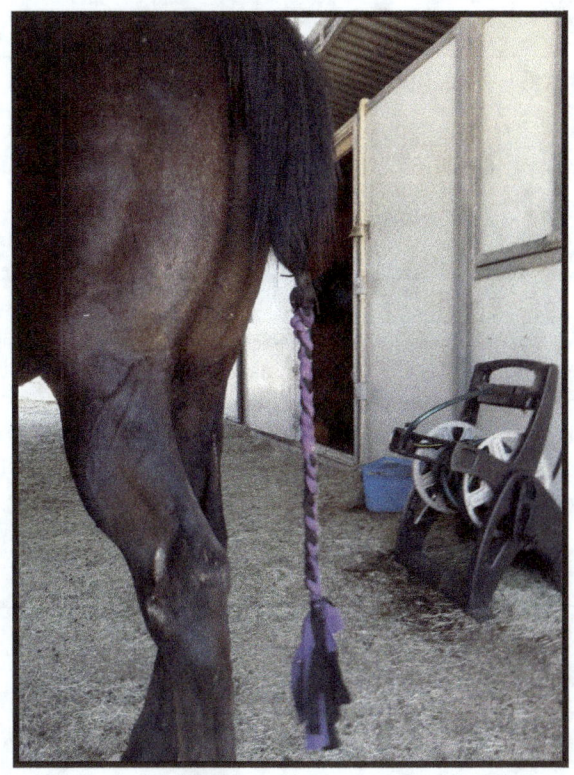

Thankfully, we humans are equipped with a proverbial "backbone." But when we fail to use it, we become tagged as "spineless." Sometimes the similarities amaze me when I compare the function of a horse's tail to courage in humans. Sometimes life's little (and big) annoyances simply require us to hold our heads high and rely on our "backbone" to swat that pesky problem out of our world. Otherwise, we end up tucking our tail between our legs and continuing to be the victim of our own spineless behavior.

"There is something about the outside of a horse that is good for the inside of a man."

Winston Churchill

The Bare Naked Truth

Recently, I've taken up riding Jr bareback. I have to say I LOVE IT! There is such a difference in connectivity. I can feel his every little twitch, and I am certain so can Jr. He also seems so much more relaxed. I, of course, only do this when I ride with Terri simply for safety reasons. It would be a disaster if I was out alone and Jr decided to challenge my comfort level. All and all, if safety were not an issue, I'd never use a saddle again! There is something so simple about removing the protective covering of a saddle and stirrups; it's not reckless or careless, but unguarded and free. I am thankful I threw caution to the wind in exchange for this experience. Aside from the lack of leather between us, what has left an impression on me is how strong the communication is between us. The first time I rode bareback, there were more words spoken between us than on any previous rides. What could be better?

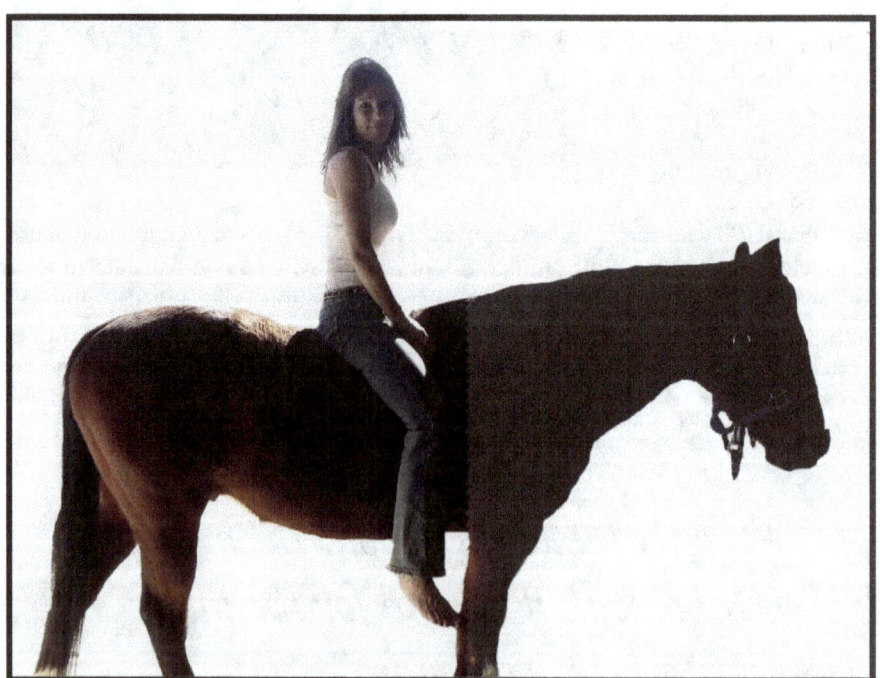

The bare naked truth . . . no barriers, nothing to hide, nothing to distort perfect wordless communication. It amazes me how even white lies or lies by omission can strip away a person's confidence and break the strongest connections. It's like putting a saddle on a horse's back. Lying takes learning a skill and extra effort to communicate, and it involves learning how to speak and remembering what to say. People are not horses. Learned behaviors and remembering stories to communicate with each other should never be the premise of any relationship, whether family or friends. It's no wonder we live in a world of neurotic, self-conscious, untrusting souls. Some people spend so much time trying too hard to live an "honest" life that they can no longer see the truth between the lies. Their lies became their reality and it's actually very sad. Yet, we find reasons to justify our lack of transparency, be those noble in our minds or simply trying to mold others' perception of us. The bare naked truth. Why is it we sacrifice the long-term benefits for a temporary moment of whatever we think we gain by forsaking it? Is it really worth it in the end?

"When your horse follows you without being asked, when he rubs his head on yours, and when you look at him and feel a tingle down your spine... you know you are loved."

John Lyons

No Bucking Way

It's been over a year since Jr and I had our first "dance" and rides have become more like Dancing with the Stars than a battle of our wills. Recently, for some reason unbeknownst to me, Jr had a momentary lapse of reasoning and decided to remind me that he in fact outweighs me by about 1,000 lbs. and is actually an animal. With the way we communicate, it is easy to forget that, with one good buck, he could actually break me into a lot of little pieces.

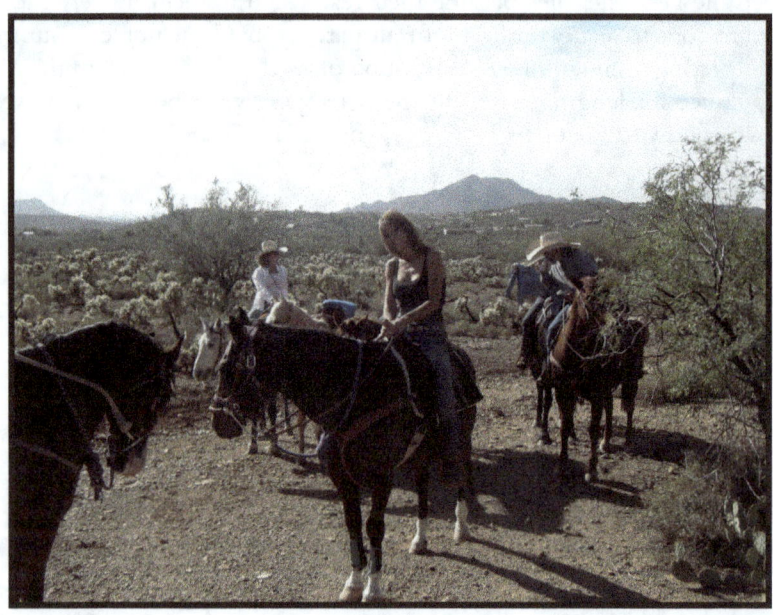

For weeks prior to this experience, I had been riding bareback. But the night before, a friend reminded me of the dangers of such riding. So I was a little cautious and saddled up. Good thing I did! As I took my friend Becca out for a casual, leisurely ride, things were going great! All the horses were well behaved until halfway into the little park we rode through. There is no explanation for Jr's outburst of uncontrollable, punk-ass bucking attitude., but suddenly it was there! I think I shocked Becca as she witnessed all 115 pounds of Robin's wrath unleashed on her beloved beast with a firm, "No bucking way! We are not bucking doing this!" proclamation as I held the reigns and went round and round in circles. Then, amazingly, all the world was at peace once again from that point on.

Horses and humans do have some things in common, one being our propensity to repeat behaviors despite negative consequences. This moment in time with Jr actually encouraged me a little as I found that my immediate response was motivated by self-preservation. On a horse you need to protect yourself physically; with human behavior, however, the mental and emotional impact of repeated harmful behavior can leave irreparable damage that can change your life forever. In a moment like that, we must muster up the courage to simply say "No bucking way," do a 360, and regain our sense of direction. Finding peace in your world sometimes can only come by a force far greater than a casual, leisurely approach. Just grab the reigns and, with determination, fearlessly head in the direction of your chosen destination. Let no bucking thing stop you!

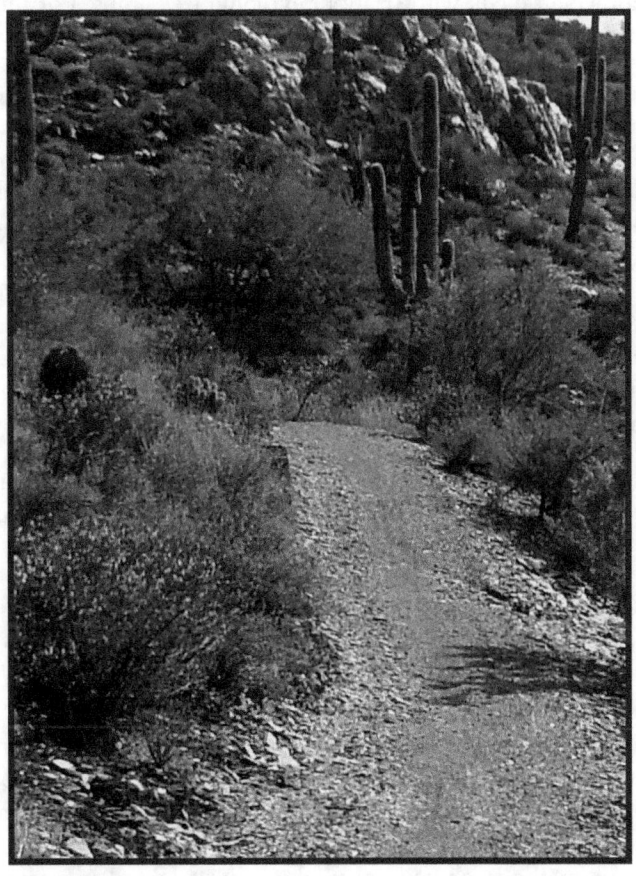

Scratch That Itch

With the summer heat, it had been several weeks since I'd been able to ride for more than an hour, but, finally, Jr and I were able to take a wonderful long ride in the middle of the desert! It was still a little steamy but certainly bearable for horse and rider.

Earlier that day, while doing morning chores, I felt very warm from the humidity (23% for all my Illinois family), so I decided to work in my blue jeans and bikini top. After that, we just saddled up and hit the trail, but I completely forgot to throw my top over my bathing suit! As we were heading down the trail, I had a nice little talk with Jr about avoiding tree limbs. For the first hour or two, he seemed to be doing great!

We rode hard with a lot of cantering and running. It was a much-needed break from the hectic life I had been living the previous few months. Thankfully, Jr was well behaved and our avoidance of shrubbery kept me free from scratches and embedded thorns. Until the second half of our ride, that is! Jr suddenly started walking right through bushes! I was bewildered! What the heck are we doing, my dear horse? Terri noticed this and we giggled with silly wonderment trying to figure out why on earth he was behaving this way. But then, Terri noticed the sweat and caked-on dirt under Jr's saddle pad and thought he might be itchy. I stopped and scratched him there, and he just moved his head around is sheer joy. My boy was simply itchy and was trying to use bushes to scratch his itch.

Scratching and itching are peculiar things. We all get them, literally and figuratively. The problem is not scratching that itch, but rather the method we choose to use as a solution. As with Jr, my too-long-for-riding fingernails provided him with some much-needed relief, whereas the shrubbery he tried to use could have hurt both him and me. One needs to be very careful when choosing the relief when that doggone itch gets hold of you. Before you know it, one thing leads to another, you're completely off the beaten path, the soothing relief seems too good to be true, and suddenly you've got poison ivy from rolling around in a place you never should have been to begin with. We all know poison ivy is contagious. It infects everyone you come in contact with, so don't think you'll be the only one affected. Scratching that itch can't be one of those live-in-the moment kind of things. You need to think about the effects of your methods or you can make a not-so-good moment become a long-term disaster.

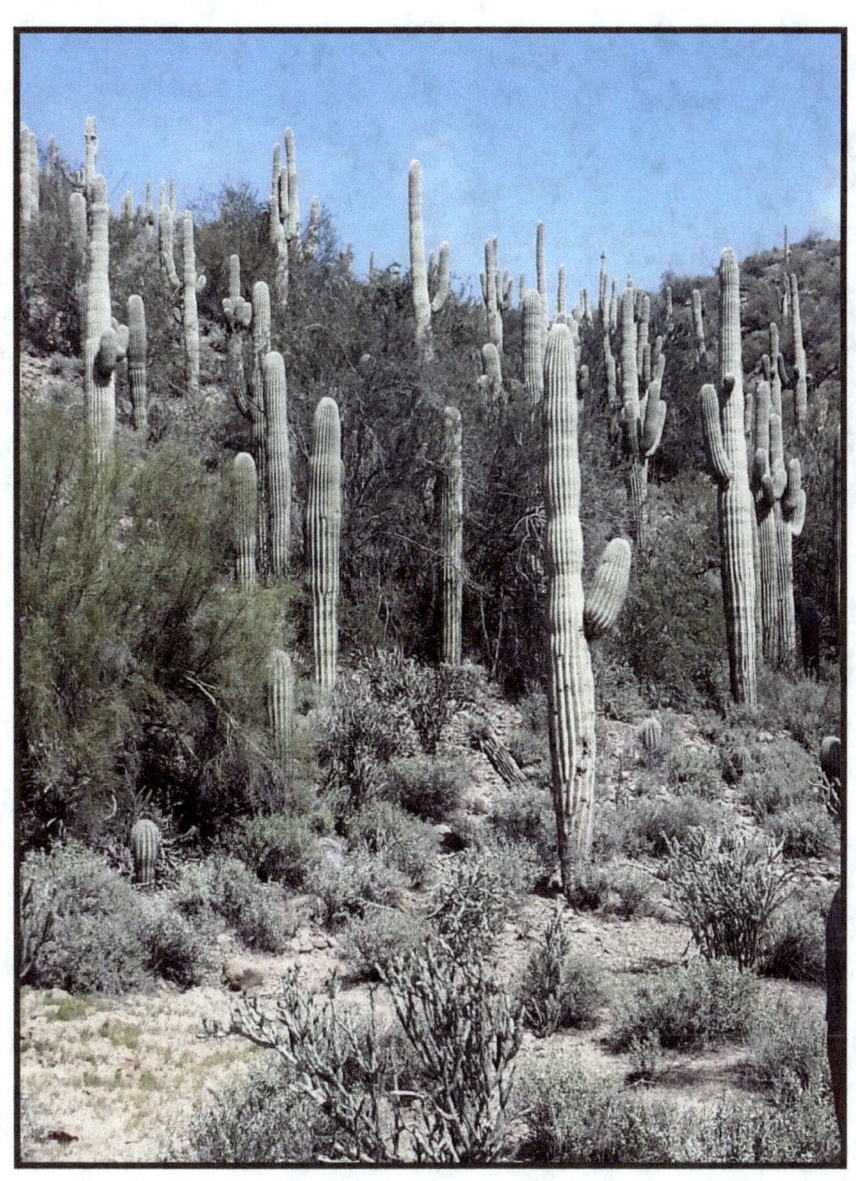

Bells and Whistles

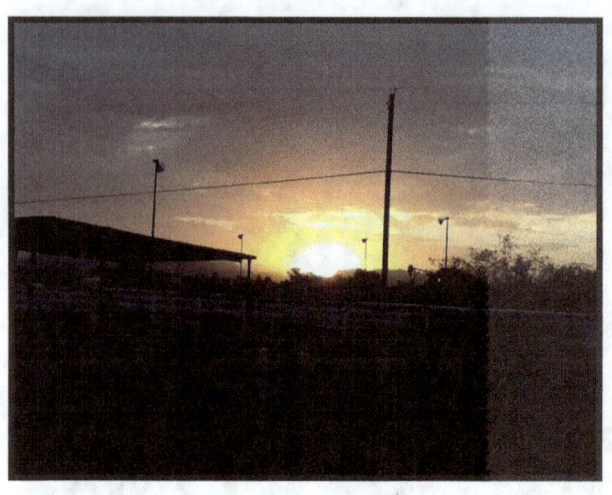

Hot, summer Sundays pretty much consist of the same routine for me. I get up before sunrise, go to the ranch, feed the animals, and do chores. A typical day of Sunday chores is to feed first because everyone is STARVING! Then, while they happily eat, I pick up the pooper scooper tools and water bucket scrubbers. This may not sound like a big chore, but we have six horses, a pony, and two goats. So, this chore can take a few hours on most days. I really don't mind; it's actually therapeutic is some ways, especially when it's very quiet and the sun is rising. No bells and whistles, just an occasional rooster crowing and the sound of happy animals eating.

What?!?! No bells and whistles? No Internet games, no Facebook, no texting? Really? Some would find that insane, simply crazy to not have immediate access to their virtual friends in the cyber and cell world! What was life like before all this technology? Don't get me wrong, I appreciate technology, but there is a fine line between appreciation and dependency. With all these great tools available to us, we have lost touch with the beauty of discovering reality. Reality sucks to so many because the bells and whistles of an imaginary world that stimulate the ego is like fast food . . . made to order and providing instant gratification. There is a control over every word and every image they see and put out there. This control takes control and becomes a driving force to be reckoned with.

What has been forgotten with all the technological advancements is that it comes with a responsibility to be balanced. Unfortunately, so few are capable of handling the responsibility that they become lost in a world that has no true feelings; at some point, they willingly forfeit real live beings around them to indulge in the technology. It's sad, really, but I guess it's the way of our world now.

I don't have to choose between the two. But if I did, I would leave the bells and whistles for the sights and sounds of a simpler reality where my mind is free from the distractions of a world built on airwaves and wires. Yes, you heard that from the girl who is typing this on her iPad and uploading it via wireless Internet to be stored online for future use. The key is balance; know when to turn off the computer, not be consumed with Facebook, and when to keep the phone out of reach. Reality is only as bad as you make it. If you give it a try without distraction, you might just be surprised how vivid the bells and whistles really are.

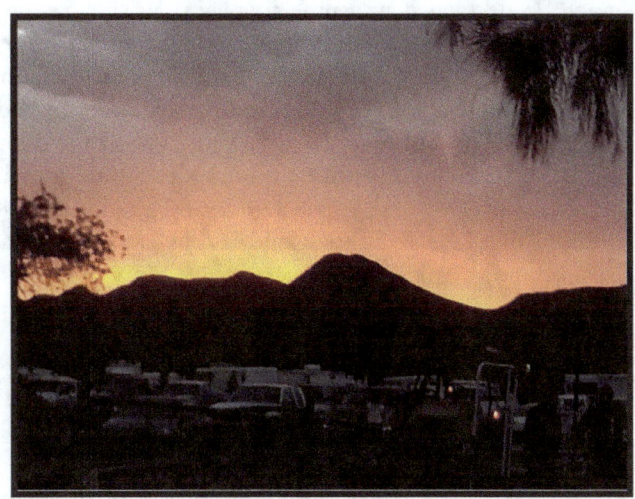

"Let a horse whisper in your ear and breathe on your heart. You will never regret it."

Author Unknown

Tickle Me Jr

One very early, beat-the-heat morning while doing the morning chores at the ranch, Jr decided it was time to play. I wasn't feeling so well, but the work needed to get done so there I was. I was doing my best to clean out water buckets with a good attitude. While my fingers were immersed in green slime and my lungs were inhaling the aroma of three-day-old horse drool, hay, and dirt after it's boiled, Jr decided he wanted to play. As I'm bent over the bucket, he puts his face in the bucket and starts to nuzzle my hair. Ok, real cute Jr. So I stop, pet him a second, giggle a little, and kiss his muzzle. Continuing my least-pleasant of all tasks, he then nuzzles my side; I jump and giggle a little more. But, no, no, he didn't stop there. Next it was my back, my leg, my arm...silly boy. I put down the scrub brush, laughed, and gave him some obviously needed attention.

Little moments like this create memories that cost nothing, only take a few minutes, and simply cannot be recreated. Yet, they make the simple things in life the most valuable. There is always work to be done, something will always come up, and money will always be needed for something "important." Just be careful with your priorities when someone you love reaches out for your time. Don't miss the memory you could be creating by taking the moment for granted. You could lose far more than you realize in the long run.

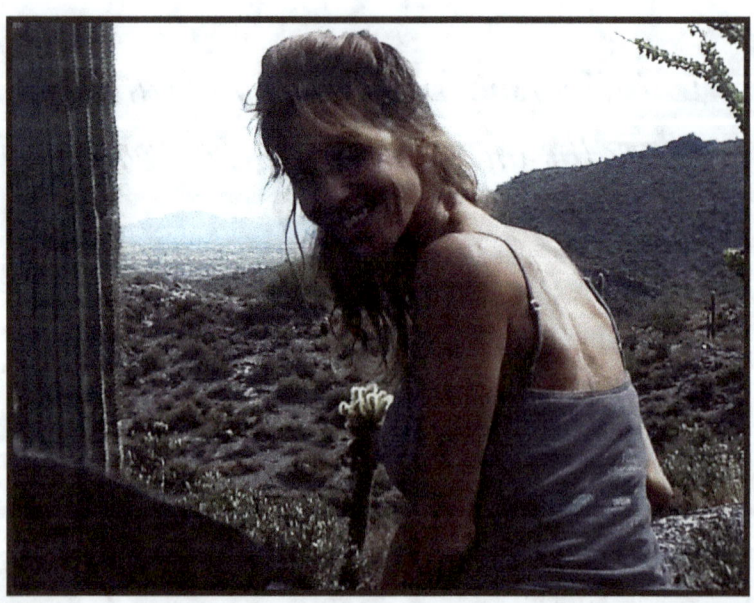

Bananas

Horses love treats! Apples and carrots are favorites with the gang for sure! One day, the president of the company where I work, Joe, was talking to me about Jr and his love for food. He wanted to know if Jr likes bananas and oranges. I realized I had no idea! The next day, Joe shows up with bananas and oranges. Of course, I did my research and found it is ok to give these to a horse, so bananas it was for a treat that night. Jr approached me all happy like he usually does, and watched with curiosity as I peeled back the banana skin. He took a big bite, and I was excited thinking we might have found a new treat! As quickly as I smile, Jr spits out the banana and sticks out his tongue! I couldn't help but laugh! I tried again and he just turned his back on me and walked away. Guess Jr doesn't like bananas. I still laugh at this whole scenario. What a silly boy.

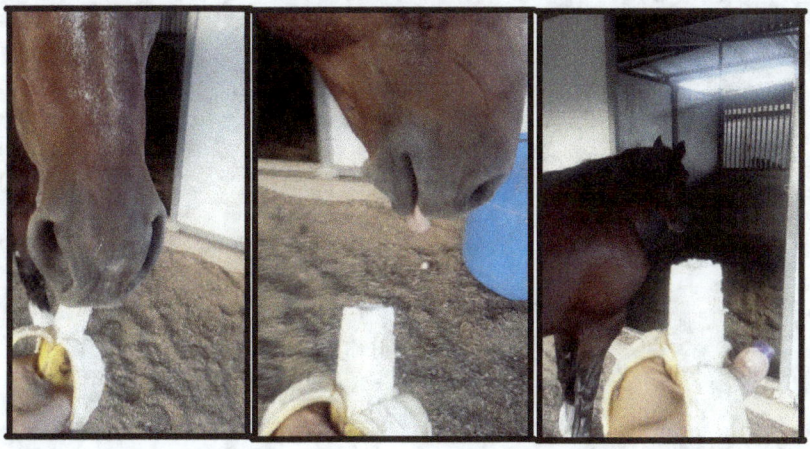

Crazy as it seems (some might say even bananas), Jr's lack of love for bananas taught me something. What is so wrong with bananas? Whatever Jr didn't like about them, he was pretty clear in his decision to just turn around and walk away. He didn't even think twice about trying it again. He wouldn't even look at me until I got rid of it! Smart horse. If something didn't work for you the first time, like Jr, it's best to just turn around, walk away, and don't even give it a second look. Jr was perfectly content with that move. I'm guessing that, even as humans, we would be too.

No Longer a Novice

Recently I took a step I had contemplated taking for a while—I saddled up another horse from the gang and took a ride. Jr handled the whole thing better than I thought he would, as did I. Black Cloud and I went out for a short ride with Terri and Cali, and it was actually a really good ride. At first it was odd being on the back of another horse, but thankfully Cloud was well behaved and followed my every lead. It was a good experience and, though Jr is still my preferred mode of horse transportation, I learned I am able to hop in the saddle of another horse and take a ride. Guess I've finally moved out of novice status and am actually a pretty decent rider. Wow!

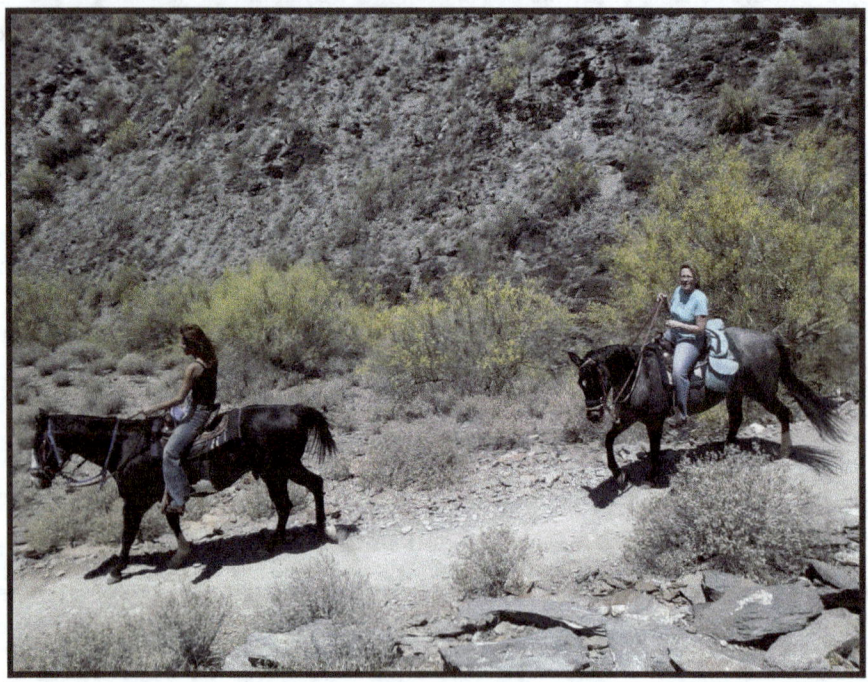

This whole journey I've been on with Jr has taught me many things about myself. Some lessons were hard to learn, some were fun. But overall I suppose I have come to realize that in life things just aren't always as they seem. We can plan, wing it, do or not do whatever we think is right, but life pays no attention to our best intentions. Life waits for no one and if you don't live it while you're alive, you have missed it. This chapter in my life as a novice rider and writer has come to an end, and though I by no means see myself as an expert, it is time to turn the page, close the book, and look forward to the next adventure.

I'm not sure where life will take me other than forward. I will still ride Jr and I will still be writing, but it's time to move past novice status and embrace what lies ahead.

To summarize my final thoughts on this subject: never take for granted the people and moments you are blessed to have. Believe in yourself even when no one else seems to. Live an honest life. And in all things, be thankful. Remember, life waits for no one; chose your path wisely and don't look back.

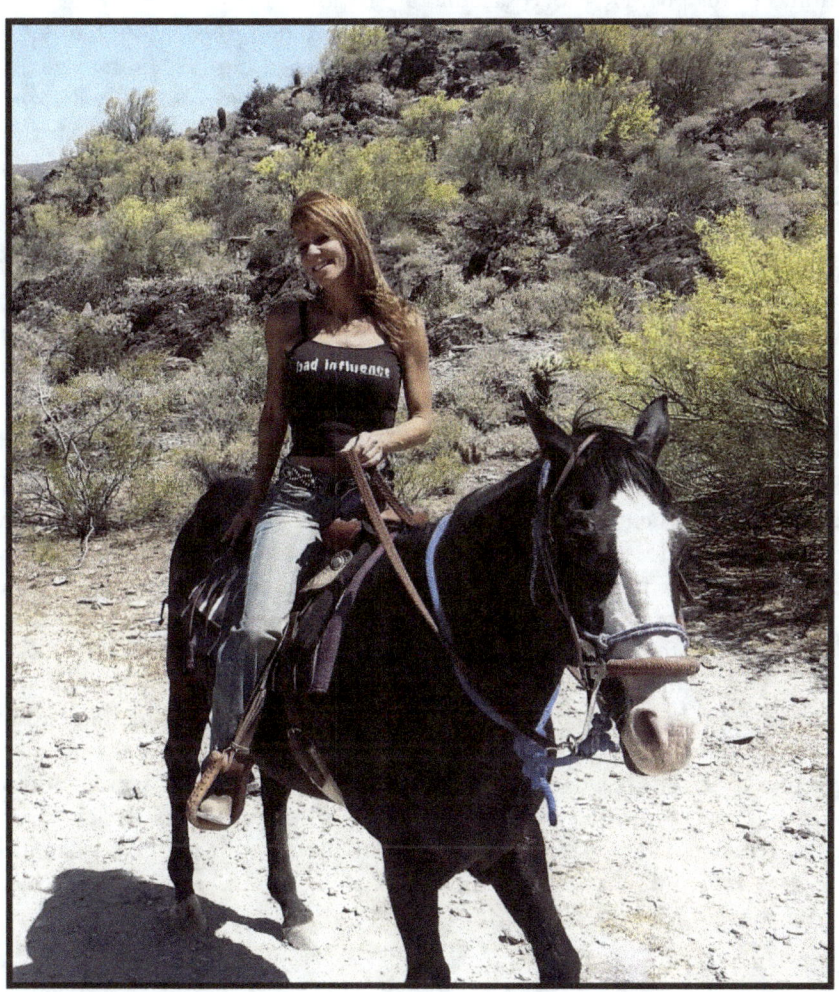

Horse-Speak

After rehabbing Jr's injury, he experienced a few rough days. One morning I noticed he was limping as he came over to greet me. When I checked his leg, it was severely inflamed. I packed it and wrapped it and he was stalled for about three months. It was heart breaking to see him so uncomfortable. I finally took him to a small round pen just to let him have a little break from the small confines of his pen. He moved around a bit with the fastest pace being a trot. After about an hour, I stalled him. The next morning he was down but got up to see me. He was limping terribly and I just hugged him. As he muzzled his nose up against my face he stilled himself for a few moments. He pulled back and just looked at me and the look was so different, none like I've seen from him before. He stepped back and got down on the ground and just looked at me. When I went down by him I just looked into his eyes and knew he was telling me it was time. As I was walking away he got up and slowly limped his way after me, and though words were not spoken, more was said in that moment through horse-speak than my human understanding could process. It had been a year of trying to rehab his old body and everything we tried didn't work. Even after the veterinarian said he was all good, his deep digital tendon was now beyond repair. Medical care, natural remedies, and all the love I could give him would not heal him. It was time to say goodbye and let go.

Saying goodbye and letting go is hard even in theory. In reality it is a long and painful process when a part of your heart and soul dies. Simply removing one from your sight does not remove them from your heart, mind, and memory. There are days the pain is as vivid as the day you parted, then as time goes on, you have more good days than bad days. One thing that doesn't go away is the bond that was forged and the history that was made. Though the loss is painful, it is an uncontrollable, sometimes unexplainable part of life. There is never a good time to say goodbye, it is rarely easy, but it is the one thing in this life that is inevitable. We must learn to accept it for what it is and allow ourselves to let go of what we know when all else has failed. It may not get easier, but we learn to rediscover who we are without what was once a part of us and redefine where we are going. We can choose to make that a daunting task or an adventure that offers things we could never imagine embracing if we remain stuck in a memory

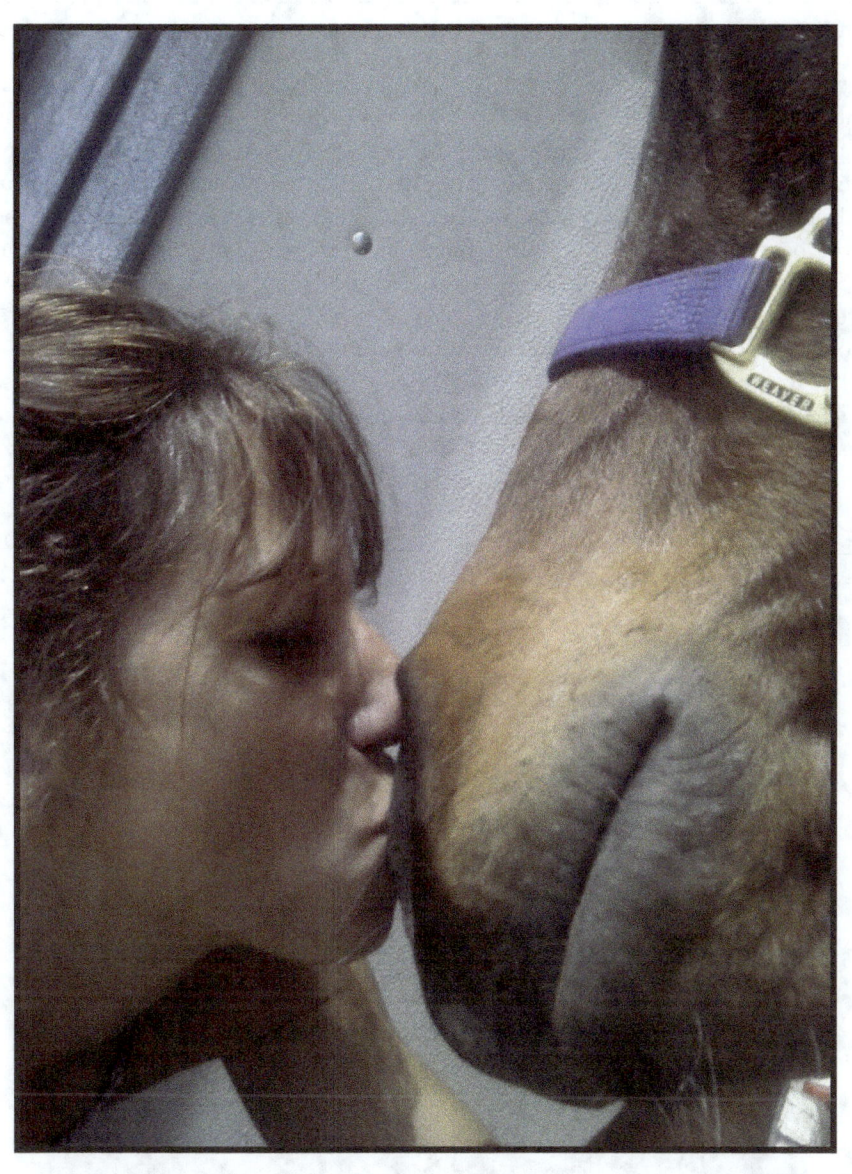

Happy Trails

Saying goodbye to your horse is an indescribable pain. When your horse is more than a means for work or show, you develop a relationship that is beyond human understanding. You invest timeless effort into creating harmonious synergy between you and your horse. The battle of your wills challenges your thought process and you learn to trust in what you do not understand. You ride together through some of the best and worst moments of your life. Your horse is always there for you, to provide comfort and rest when your soul is weary. It also teaches you how to say goodbye. Jr taught me how to grieve, how to let myself cry, and then rest to awake to a new day with acceptance for what was, what is, and what will be. There is a void in me that no other horse will ever fill, but one day there will be another horse who will teach me new life lessons. I will apply what Jr has taught me to bring me a notch above novice, and will experience even more than I can imagine now.

Happy trails Jr. I love you, I miss you, and I thank you for all you've taught me about horsemanship, myself, and life.

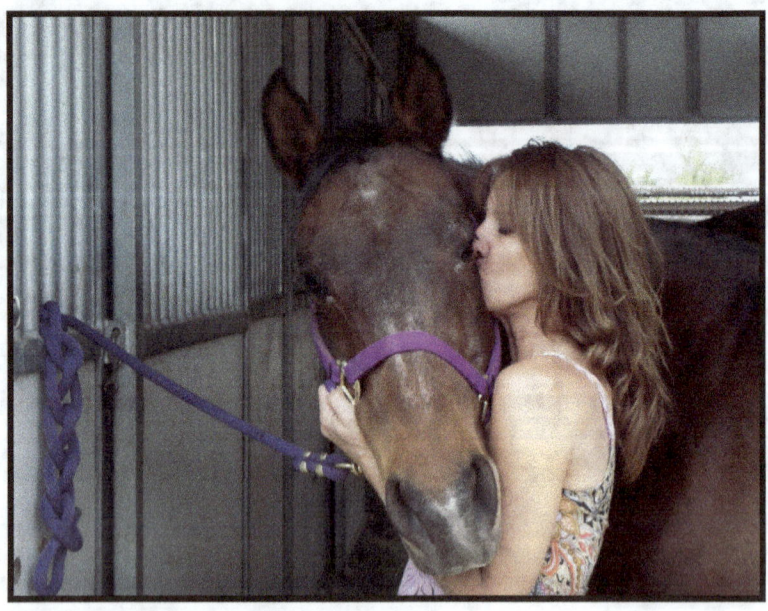

Final Thoughts

While the relationship between horse and rider may be hard for most to understand, there is a certain solitude I find when I can "ride off into the sunset" and leave my cares behind. You've read many accounts in both books of my experiences and the sometimes funny lessons I applied, but beneath the words and between the lines there have been many hard lessons learned. Jr provided a safe place for me to process my worries, be distracted from the pain, and even somehow make me smile from the inside out when my world seemed to be crumbling beneath me.

I still have moments of sadness as I look through the pages of these books, because I miss my Jr so much, but I have been blessed this year (September 2014) with a new horse adventure. I met Cherokee (an 11-year-old mare), at a horse rescue and despite having no intentions of getting another horse for a few more months (especially a mare), she chose me. She is not Jr but she is precious to me and we are creating a new synergy, new memories, and I have found myself once again on an unfamiliar trail in this thing called life.

As I stated at the beginning of this book, the end of 2013 presented many challenges, and many more I didn't even mention. The twists and turns that have brought me here have changed me, not for the better or for the worse. While my sense of direction isn't always the best, I know I will somehow get to where I need to be. I cannot say with certainty where I will go or how I will get there, but I am certain I will continue to ride this big adventure with expectancy. What do I expect? Love, laughter, and simplicity. I will enjoy the ride while I am still in the saddle; my hope for you is that you do the same.

Thank you all for sharing in my adventures with Jr.

It's been a great ride!

www.ingramcontent.com/pod-product-compliance
Lightning Source LLC
Chambersburg PA
CBHW060149200526
45165CB00023B/1562